Nowhere to Go But Up

Nowhere to Go But Up

The Power of Living in God's Love,
Rather Than Fearing God's Wrath

KEVIN E. RUFFCORN
foreword by Rick Rouse

RESOURCE *Publications* · Eugene, Oregon

NOWHERE TO GO BUT UP
The Power of Living in God's Love, Rather Than Fearing God's Wrath

Unless noted otherwise, Scripture quotations have been taken from the Holy Bible, New Revised Standard Version (NRSV). Copyright © 2015 by the National Council of the Churches of Christ in the USA. All rights reserved.

The Holy Bible, English Standard Version® (ESV®) Copyright © 2001 by Crossway, a publishing ministry of Good News Publishers. All rights reserved. ESV Text Edition: 2016

Resource Publications
An Imprint of Wipf and Stock Publishers
199 W. 8th Ave., Suite 3
Eugene, OR 97401

www.wipfandstock.com

PAPERBACK ISBN: 978-1-7252-6607-0
HARDCOVER ISBN: 978-1-7252-6605-6
EBOOK ISBN: 978-1-7252-6606-3

Manufactured in the U.S.A.   07/06/20

This book is dedicated to all of the people, both living and dead, who have experienced the judgment and marginalization of the Christian community, and have been condemned to hell—an eternity of excruciating torture and agonizing punishment—because of who they are, what they believe, or what they have done. May they rest in God's love, rejoice in God's grace, and find in their hearts the ability to forgive.

"Since the very beginning, Church history has been rife with unrest, conflict, and even bloodshed—primarily over matters of establishing orthodoxy. And with today's easy access to the annals of Church history, it's time for us . . . to rethink the *myth of orthodoxy*, and begin re-evaluating what we've been taught."[1]

1. Brazen Church, "How and When."

Contents

Foreword by Rick Rouse | ix

Preface | xi

Introduction | xvii

Prologue | 1

1   Truth and Lies—Hell and the Christian Church | 5

2   Changing Theology—Our Understanding of God is Dynamic | 24

3   A History of Hell—A Non-Biblical Church Doctrine | 31

4   Judgment in the Bible—Not Retribution and Not Everlasting | 39

5   God's Justice—Moving Toward Restoration | 50

6   Christ's Work on the Cross—No One Church Doctrine | 64

7   Breaking Down the Barriers—The Benefits of a Hell-less World | 84

Epilogue | 108

Bibliography | 111

Foreword

"Before you speak to me about your religion. First show it to me in how you treat other people; before you tell me how much you love our God, show me in how much you love all His children; before you preach to me of your passion for our faith; teach me about it through your compassion for your neighbors. In the end, I'm not as interested in what you have to tell or see as I am in how you choose to live and give."

—Senator Cory Booker

We live in a time of division and polarization when both politicians and religious leaders unabashedly use matters of faith as a weapon or wedge issue in support of their cause. Whether it be abortion, birth control, or civil liberties for people who identify as LGBTQ+, we are told that if we are not on the "right" side of scripture we are not only wrong but will face God's wrath and condemnation. This kind of arrogance and self-righteousness can lead to hate speech and discrimination. In some cases, a particular form of Christianity has become a shield to excuse one from racism and acts of terrorism against those of other faith traditions. Witness the alarming rise in acts of violence against Jews, Muslims, and migrants—not just in America but around the globe.

Where are the teachings of Jesus and other religious luminaries who have sought to bring a message of peace, love, and reconciliation among peoples? We need to rediscover what grace is all about and how both the

Old and New Testament point us to a loving and compassionate God, not an angry tyrant. We also must reclaim a sense of decency and mutual respect for one another, regardless of one's particular belief or status. At its worst, religion can be harmful and destructive; at its best, it can bring people together in a spirit of cooperation and care for all of God's creation.

This book is a journey filled with both allegory and theological reflection that seeks to understand how the biblical story can be misunderstood and how faith has been weaponized to the point where it can strike fear into, rather than comfort, the hearts of many. The author then guides the reader to find a way to restore the Gospel message to a place of prominence in our hearts and minds, so that it is indeed Good News for all. Finally, it is this Gospel of undeserved grace that propels believers to make a difference for good in our world. The words of the following hymn illustrate this well:

"Come! Open your heart! Show your mercy to all those who fear! We are called to be hope for the hopeless so hatred and blindness will be no more. . .Sing! Sing a new song! Sing of that great day when all will be one! God will reign, and we'll walk with each other as sisters and brothers united in love." (David Hass, "We Are Called," © 1988, GIA Publications, Inc.)

—REV. DR. RICK ROUSE,
　　Author of *The World is About to Turn: Mending a Nation's Broken Faith*

Preface

I am not sure when I first became aware of the concept of Hell as a place of eternal punishment. I remember I thought a lot about Hell, especially one day when I was four years old.

My family had a 1950, gunmetal blue Ford. On this particular day, my father had parked the car in the driveway close to the garage. I was playing in the area of the backyard where there was a sandbox and swing set. It was next to the driveway. Evidently, I became bored with my sandbox construction project and Tonka trucks, because I left them and wandered over to the car. I found the car unlocked, so I opened the door and crawled into the driver's seat. Taking hold of the steering wheel I suddenly imagined myself racing down a curvy country road. I swung the steering wheel this way and that way as I squealed around the turns and accelerated down the straightaways. I surprised myself at my great driving ability—I was even a better driver than my father—and he was a great driver!

Arriving at my destination, I reached over to turn off the engine, like I had seen my father do hundreds of times before. The keys were not in the ignition, but there was a bright, silver button on the dash (I found out later it was called the "starter button"). I pushed the button and the car lurched forward into the garage wall. Though I was unharmed, I was terribly scared. (I do not recall if there were any contents in my pants that betrayed the level of my fear.)

My mother and father heard the bang and rushed to see what had happened. They quickly realized what I had done when they saw me emerge from the car. They experienced one of those parental moments—they were overjoyed I had not been hurt, yet they were very angry that I had crashed the car. After hugs and a quick examination, I received the scolding of my young life and was sent, like Dennis the Menace, to sit on my small chair in the corner of the kitchen, to contemplate the magnitude of my sinful actions. It was then that I thought a lot about Hell and wondered if I would ever receive a reprieve. (If you are wondering about the extent of the damage that occurred, the front metal bumper of the car chipped a block in the garage's concrete wall. That block scratched the point of the bumper. The damage was almost unnoticeable.)

My family was not overly religious. Still, I was regularly dropped off at Sunday school and I endured a two year educational/hazing process called confirmation. Between classes and the occasional worship services we attended, I heard quite a lot about Hell and the threat of being separated from God and punished for eternity.

To be fair, I also heard about God's grace. I was raised in the Lutheran Church, which is a denomination that celebrates that humankind has been saved by grace through faith and that our salvation is a gift from God. The congregation in which I was raised, though, was a part of the pietistic branch of Lutheranism. Though we heard about grace, we were also told we needed to have a personal relationship with Jesus. Evidence of this relationship was that we didn't dance, play cards, cuss, smoke, chew, drink, or view risqué movies. To engage in any of these activities risked the demise of our relationship with Jesus and the loss of our salvation. The path toward Hell loomed before us.

We understood that we had received faith and salvation as a gift from God because we were God's chosen people. People who believed differently than we did, even though they called themselves Christians, were not saved. Those who were members of different faiths were not saved. Men, women, and children who lived in distant parts of the world and who had never heard about Jesus were not saved. In other words, most people on the face of the earth were going to Hell and would experience an eternity of torture and punishment. Our calling, as God's chosen ones, was to tell others about Jesus so they could receive faith and escape the threat of Hell.

Over the years, my journey of faith has led me far away from this world view. Today I identify myself as a practical theologian. Others would call me a parish pastor (retired). I attended Luther Theological Seminary in St. Paul, Minnesota and received my MDiv. Years later I earned my doctorate (DMin.) from Asbury Theological Seminary in Wilmore, Kentucky. For over forty years, as a parish pastor, I helped people apply the teachings of Jesus to their everyday lives. During those years, I became increasingly convinced that the focus of Jesus's teachings was not on the avoidance of Hell in the life to come, but rather the ability to live in the reality of God's kingdom in our everyday lives.

For example, a scribe approaches Jesus and asks him what the greatest commandment is. Jesus sums up the Ten Commandments with these words: "You shall love the Lord your God with all your heart, and with all your soul, and with all your mind. This is the greatest and first commandment. And a second is like it: You shall love your neighbor as yourself" (Matt 22:37–39). When the Lord gave the Israelites the Ten Commandments at Mount Sinai, God's relationship with God's children had already been established. God had identified the enslaved Israelites as "my people" when God spoke to Moses at the burning bush. So, Jesus's response is not meant to be a way to earn God's love, nor is it instructions on how to obtain a "Get Out of Hell Free" pass. Instead, Jesus's words are an invitation to a lifestyle. When we realize God's love for us and celebrate that love through our gratitude and service, we walk in God's kingdom. Overflowing with God's love and ministering to the needs of others enables us to glimpse heaven on earth.

In Matthew 18, Peter asks Jesus how many times he should forgive a person who sins against him (Matt 18:21–22). Jesus's reply can be summed up "Never stop forgiving someone." Again, this is not advice on how to avoid Hell in the next life. It is, rather, sage guidance on how to avoid our self-made, present-day hells of holding grudges, nursing old wounds, and stoking the fires of hate in this life.

Concepts of hell run the gamut in the minds of modern-day Christians. Many don't give much thought to hell and its possible consequences—nor do they spend much time reflecting on the magnificence of heaven. For others, hell becomes real when they believe they have committed an unforgivable sin. These might include (but aren't limited to) adultery, addiction, the breaking of a law, or being the cause of a crippling or fatal accident. Though others may forgive them, they cannot forgive themselves and cannot understand how God could forgive them either. They believe, in their hearts, that eternal torture and punishment befits their sin.

Whatever individual Christians believe, condemnation and eternal punishment in Hell is still a doctrine of the Christian Church. Several branches of the Christian Church express their belief that Jesus descended into Hell; they affirm this every time they worship and proclaim their faith in the words of the Apostles' Creed. Other groups of Christians struggle with the idea of purgatory and making themselves and their loved ones worthy of avoiding Hell and entering Heaven. If pastors (like me) don't preach on hell and the dire consequences it holds, one or two parishioners are certain to make an appointment in order to ask why we are neglecting such an important doctrine.

A significant portion of Christians is encouraged to share their faith with their family, friends, neighbors, and co-workers. Their hope is that these people will accept Jesus as their Lord and Savior and thus escape the threat of hell and an afterlife of eternal punishment. There are also many Christians who anticipate the imminent return of Jesus. His return will set off a chain of events that will eventually lead to the judgment of all people. At this judgment, some will be declared righteous and enter into Heaven. Many, however, will be condemned and cast into Hell.

I was reminded of the power of the doctrine of hell and eternal punishment a few years ago. Attending a meeting of an LGBTQ Alliance group, I heard several stories of young people—teenagers—"coming out" and identifying who they were to their family and friends. Many of these young people were raised in families that identified themselves as Christian. The themes of their stories were all similar. When they came out to their parents, they were rejected. Their parents condemned who they were, announced they were living in sin, and proclaimed that they were going to Hell because they were not *normal*. Personally, I cannot imagine how any loving parent could tell their child that he or she is going to Hell. Yet, that is exactly what happened.

The power of rejection and condemnation had a devastating effect on those young people. They were driven out of their families and they rejected the wrathful god who, they were told, rejected them. These young people were alone and in search of a community that would accept them. Thankfully, they found the Alliance. In that fellowship, they found love and acceptance, and they heard the good news that God loved them and made them just the way God wanted them to be.

The effects of the church's doctrine of hell and eternal condemnation cannot be ignored. Followers of Jesus have been commissioned to continue Jesus's ministry of sharing God's love and grace. We have been entrusted to proclaim the good news (gospel) that the life, death, and resurrection of Jesus reconciled all of humankind to this God of love—their creator. Their reconciliation enables humankind to live in the reality of God's presence and power—God's kingdom.

Our words and actions, however, are jumbled and distorted by the church's doctrine of hell and its accompanying god of judgment and wrath. Compounding its devilish effects is the doctrine's propensity to judge and to separate the righteous from the unrighteous and the good from the bad. Instead of unifying us as God's beloved children—as Jesus intended—hell drives a wedge between us.

It is time for us to reexamine the doctrine of hell and eternal condemnation. We need to see where the doctrine had its roots, how it developed, and why it became so widespread throughout the church. When we do this, I am confident that we will come to the conclusion that the doctrine of hell is a figment of the church's theological imagination. The doctrine has no place in the life of the church nor in the proclamation of the gospel of Jesus Christ.

Once we do this, it will be necessary for us to take a second step and imagine what life will be like without hell. This will require a fresh understanding of Jesus's saving work in his life, death, and resurrection. The second step will also challenge us to see the world—the people of the world—from a new perspective. Though this view of the world may be new to us, it is the understanding of people that Jesus demonstrated during his time on earth. It is the knowledge that we are all beloved children of God. Despite our differences, we are all family.

This fresh perspective is imperative for us to incorporate into our lives as we experience the increased diversity in our lives. Knowing that we are all God's children encourages us to focus on our similarities and not on our differences. It lessens or eliminates the fear of others by helping us realize that it is no longer *us* and *them*, but rather *we*. Living in the reality that through Jesus's life, death, and resurrection, we have all been reconciled to the God of love who empowers us to celebrate that there is nowhere to go but up!

Introduction

There are many fine books that question the existence of Hell and the threat of eternal condemnation. Another group of writings advocates for the acceptance of universal salvation. I have used a few books from both groups to bolster my arguments, which are presented in this book. *Nowhere to Go but Up*, however, does not seek to add to the information in these genres. Rather, the book only repeats some of the information they contain.

It is hoped that enough information has been gathered and presented to the readers that they will reach the conclusion that hell is a figment of the church's theological imagination. When this information is presented, readers will see the human side of the church—both good and bad. I do not believe that in doing this I have cast a harsh light on the church, but rather a realistic light. Christians have always affirmed that the church is both human and divine. In the past, though, the emphasis has been placed on the movement and inspiration of the Holy Spirit. The personal interplay, political intrigue, and struggle for power and control of church leaders have been downplayed. While the presence of the Holy Spirit is not denied, in the following pages the focus of the discussion is on the words and actions of the human element.

The writers who have questioned the existence of Hell and argued against the scriptural underpinnings for eternal punishment have done solid research and presented valid points to support their positions. A person can disagree with their conclusions, but their arguments demand serious consideration and cannot be sloughed off as mere foolishness. I believe, however, these authors have not gone far enough. When I read there is no hell and ruminate on the possibility of universal salvation, a question pops into my mind: "If this is so, then what did Jesus accomplish on the cross?" In the books I have read, this question has not been adequately addressed.

The penal substitutionary theory of atonement is currently in vogue. This theory (I prefer the word "motif") proclaims that sinless Jesus died for sinful humankind because the wages of sin is death (Rom 6:23). Jesus died so that we might live. All we need to do is confess our sinfulness, place our faith in Jesus, and receive him as our Lord and Savior; we will then escape the ravages of Hell. Many Biblical scholars and theologians are critical of the penal substitutionary theory of atonement and consider it an inaccurate and inadequate understanding of the atonement. The absence of hell and the reality of universal salvation bolster their arguments against the theory, to say the least. The question remains, though. "Why did Jesus need to be crucified?"

Unlike its doctrine of hell, the church does not have one atonement motif. Several motifs have been popular throughout the centuries. This book reviews the main motifs that have appeared throughout two millennia of the church's history. The point is made that people do not need to live with just one motif and reject others. As people strive to understand the life, death, and resurrection of Jesus and allow its truth to be incorporated into their lives, they do not need to limit themselves to an either/or view of the atonement. Rather, they can embrace a both/and perspective. Doing so maintains the potential of opening up a whole new way of life.

The church's focus on Hell and its effects has been centered on the afterlife; how hell has affected the everyday lives of people has been neglected. Hell has cast a dark shadow over the shining light of the gospel of Jesus Christ. By his life, death, and resurrection, Jesus proclaimed that God is a God of love. The doctrine of hell portrays God as a judgmental and wrathful being. Jesus, in his life, death, and resurrection, demonstrated that all people—sick, demon-possessed, unclean, and marginalized—were children of God. The doctrine of hell separates and divides. There are the righteous/ unrighteous, saved/unsaved, good/bad, right/wrong, and them/us.

Without Hell, the good news of God's love and grace can shine brightly in our lives. *Nowhere to Go but Up* paints a picture of the possibilities that loom before us as we live in the reality that all humankind (and all of creation) is beloved of God. We are all children of God. There is no *us* and *them*. There is only *we*. When this truth revolutionizes our lives, there truly is *Nowhere to Go but Up*!

Prologue

The sun caressed the small town in its late spring glow. By late morning it had warmed the air to a shirt-sleeve temp. A light breeze spread the fragrance of lilacs across the landscape of well-trimmed lawns and modest homes. Residents were outside enjoying the day. Some were strolling along, while others tended to yard chores or hurried to their next appointment. The town could have been a knock-off of Garrison Keillor's imaginary village of Lake Wobegon. Keillor always introduced his stories of the town by saying, "All the women were strong, all the men were good-looking, and all the children were above average." That was, at least, Lydia's first impression of the community as she wandered down the sidewalk looking into shop windows and greeting total strangers with a cheery "Hi!" She had come into town to be a part of her nephew's baptism. The child's parents had asked Lydia to be one of the child's godparents.

Lydia paused, leaned against a lamppost, and surveyed the scene around her. Despite the sunshine, warm temperature, and pleasant breeze, something was amiss. Her brow furrowed as she inspected the area, trying to find the piece that was out of place or the object that didn't belong. Lydia had almost given up and resumed her walk when it hit her. It was the people's eyes—they didn't match the smiles that many of the people sported.

Lydia's mind flashed back to a time several years ago when she and her family were hunkered down in a storm cellar, riding out a series of tornadoes. She sat on her mother's lap. Her mother stroked a wayward strand of hair and placed it behind Lydia's ear. She smiled. "It will be okay," she assured her children. Her eyes didn't match her smile, though. They betrayed her worry and fear.

That's the piece that didn't match the rest of the scene. The people smiled, but their eyes were anxious and foreboding. Making a mental note of her impression, Lydia continued on her tour of the town.

Several blocks passed under Lydia's feet before she turned a corner, intending to return to her brother's home. The scene before her changed. It was as if she'd walked off a sound stage and into the mess behind the backdrops. A large house stood before her. Unlike the other homes, this one was shabby. The paint was peeling, windows were broken, and shutters hung at odd angles. The lawn was brown—long past due for a mowing and filled with weeds. Trees were dead and shrubs looked jagged with untrimmed branches. The property was surrounded by a rusting, saggy cyclone fence complete with weather-worn "No Trespassing" signs.

Lydia could have sworn the warm glow of the sun dimmed. The breeze picked up and blew in an acrid smell of death and decay. There was a sinister quality to the house. It radiated a sense of evil. The longer Lydia spent surveying the house and grounds, the more uncomfortable she became. The hairs on the back of her neck began to rise. When she turned to leave, Lydia noticed that, unlike the sidewalks a few blocks away with people walking to and fro, the sidewalk around this house was devoid of life. Lydia picked up her pace, determined to put as much distance between her and the house as soon as possible.

"Hello," rang out from the kitchen when Lydia arrived back at her brother's home. A "How was your walk?" was cut short when Lydia entered the kitchen and her brother saw her.

"What happened?" he questioned with concern in his voice, "You look upset; like you saw a ghost."

Lydia furrowed her eyebrows and sighed. "Maybe I did," she replied. She then related to her brother what she had seen and felt.

"I'll have to give some thought to the anxious eyes," her brother said thoughtfully. "The house . . . that's the old Malmstad place," he said with a wave of his hand. "That house has been an eyesore and blight on the community for decades." He slid his chair back from the kitchen table, got up, and headed toward the coffeemaker. Filling a cup with the steaming brew, he handed the mug to Lydia. "Sit down and enjoy a good cup of my coffee. It's Peruvian. I think you'll like it."

Lydia accepted the mug and, holding it in both hands, brought it to her lips and took a sip. "Ummm, it is good." She took another sip, placed the mug on the table and slid into a chair and turned her attention to what her brother was saying.

"The Malmstads were a prominent family in town about seventy or eighty years ago. He was a banker. I understand that he had a beautiful wife and two children—a boy in his early teens and a girl a few years younger. There were some hard economic times, and Malmstad had to foreclose on several farms. You can imagine that he wasn't a well-liked man around town. In fact, there were threats to his life, but no one took them seriously."

Lydia's brother sipped a little coffee before continuing. "One fall night—I actually think it was Halloween—someone broke into the house and killed the entire family. They dismembered the bodies and piled the pieces up in the parlor. Malmstad, of course, didn't show up at the bank the next day and, when he couldn't be reached by phone, the head teller went over to check things out. He came across the gruesome site, threw up his breakfast, and called the police."

"Local law enforcement called in the State Police. Some people say that even the FBI was involved in the manhunt. They never found any suspects, though. Everyone had a few suspicions as to who did it, but the most likely suspects all had rock-solid alibis. To this day it's one of those unsolved mysteries. I'm surprised they haven't made a movie out of what happened. Of course, with that type of history, no one wants to buy the house. It's just been allowed to deteriorate."

"I'm surprised they haven't torn it down and made it into a park or something," Lydia said.

"Oh, they've tried. There've been petitions and referendums but, for some reason, the city officials haven't been able to tear the place down. They can't fix it up either. They can only watch it become more of an eyesore. In the meantime, stories abound about how the house is haunted. The spirits of the family members must be restless until their murderer is found. There are a couple of stories of people who had been seen around the Malmstad place, but they disappeared and were never heard about again. Though hardly anyone pays attention to those stories, you won't find many people near the Malmstad place—especially at night."

Lydia's brother paused in thought and a frown appeared on his face. "You know . . . recently there's been an increase in illegal drugs around town. There have also been some rumors that a gang is trying to claim the town as part of its "turf." With his fingers, he made the sign of quotation marks in the air. "The old Malmstad place keeps being mentioned as the probable center for such activities; that may be the cause of some of the anxiety that you noticed."

Lydia's brother shrugged his shoulders. Switching to a lighter note, he snickered, "Some parents have used the Malmstad place to their advantage, though. If they have problems with their kids being disruptive and not be-having, all they need to do is to threaten to bring their kids to the Malmstad place for the night. A threat like that is very effective in quieting the children down."

"I can only imagine," replied Lydia with a grin, blowing on her coffee before taking another sip. "It is too bad, though. The house and lot are so disgusting and there is an oppressiveness—almost an evil presence—about the site. It casts a pallor on the entire community. Life in this town would be so much better without the Malmstad place," Lydia opined.

Many communities have houses like the Malmstad place—places that have the reputation of being haunted and dangerous. They reek of evil, and they cast a cloud of gloom over the community. Even the church tells us of such a place. It's called Hell. The presence and threat of Hell have robbed God's children of the assurance of God's love for them. The prospect of Hell has drained lives of happiness, inspired profound grief, and, for many, eliminated the possibility of experiencing lives that are abundant and free and with a peace that passes all understanding.

1

Truth and Lies

Hell and the Christian Church

THE GOSPEL OF LOVE—30 TO 200 CE

Hell has not always played as dominant a role in Christian theology as it does today. In fact, those first Christians would be amazed and perhaps appalled at the attention hell is currently receiving, as we shall see.

The four gospels in the canon of the New Testament convey the message that the disciples and other followers of Jesus were to continue Jesus's ministry. They were to be witnesses to Jesus's life, death, and resurrection. The world-transforming truth that the kingdom of God has arrived through the person of Jesus was something the disciples and followers of Jesus were to declare through their words and actions.

Mark is blatant in this perspective. He begins his gospel with the words, "The beginning of the good news of Jesus Christ, the Son of God" (Mark 1:1). Most Biblical scholars understand the words of verse 1 to be the title of Mark's gospel. The story of Jesus: his miracles, message, death, and resurrection are only the beginning of the good news. It is chapter one. The Holy Spirit was working through Jesus ever since the Spirit. descended upon Jesus at the time of his baptism (Mark 1:9–11). It was the Spirit who inspired Jesus's self-understanding that "the Son of Man came not to be served but to serve, and to give his life a ransom for many" (Mark 10:45). She continued her work in the life of the church as chapter 2 of the "Good News of Jesus

Christ the Son of God," was written. The Spirit carries on her work in and through the church in all of the subsequent chapters.

Like many good writers, Mark ends his story with a bit of a cliff hanger. When the three women, Mary Magdalene, Mary the mother of James, and Salome enter the tomb on the morning of the first Easter, they encounter a young man dressed in a white robe (Mark 16:5). This young man tells them not to be alarmed. He declares to the three women that Jesus has been raised and is no longer in the tomb. The young man then orders the women to go and tell Jesus's disciples and Peter that Jesus will meet them in Galilee. Mark's story ends abruptly with the women fleeing the tomb, overwhelmed with terror and amazement. The women were so afraid that they didn't tell anyone what had happened. The story could have ended at chapter 1. The readers of Mark's gospel know, however, that the silence of the women did not last. Eventually, the women told the disciples, the disciples began to tell others, and the truth spread. The kingdom of God, from that time on, has expanded one life at a time.

Matthew and Luke, the other two synoptic gospels, have their own perspective on what the followers of Jesus were called to do following Jesus's ascension. During the last week of his life on earth, what we now call Holy Week, Matthew records a parable that Jesus tells concerning the judgment of the nations (Matt 25:31–46). The end of time has come and the nations are gathered before the throne of God. The people are separated into two groups—the righteous and the unrighteous. Those who were listening to Jesus would assume that the righteous were those people who were doing religious things like keeping the Sabbath, eating kosher food, offering sacrifices, and praying. The unrighteous would be those people who were too caught up in life to do what was pleasing to God. The parable turns the tables, however. In this parable, the unrighteous are those people who were so caught up in religious living they didn't respond to the needs of those who were hungry, thirsty, naked, strangers, sick, or in prison. The people who are called righteous in this parable are those who saw the needs around them and responded to those needs. The central theme of the parable is that the followers of Jesus are to care for the needs of others similar to the way Jesus cared for others during his earthly ministry. By doing this, the followers of Jesus are not only loving their neighbors as themselves; they are also loving God with all of their heart, soul, mind, and strength. As Jesus tells them, "Truly I tell you, just as you did it to one of the least of these who are members of my family, you did it to me" (Matt 25:40).

Shortly after hearing this parable and receiving these instructions, Jesus is betrayed, arrested, and taken from the disciples. The disciples' interaction with Jesus is limited until after Jesus's resurrection when the disciples meet him in Galilee before his ascension. Before he leaves the disciples, Jesus commissions them and all of his followers with the words, "All authority in heaven and on earth has been given to me. Go therefore and make disciples of all nations, baptizing them in the name of the Father and of the Son and of the Holy Spirit, and teaching them to obey everything that I have commanded you. And remember, I am with you always, to the end of the age" (Matt 28:18–20). The marching orders are clear. Followers of Jesus are to gather people into the community of God's family (the kingdom of God) and teach these new followers to live in response to God's love and grace by sharing their blessings and ministering to the needs of others. The emphasis was not on asserting certain doctrinal beliefs but in living lives of love and grace.

Luke echoes Matthew's gospel. Throughout Luke's gospel, Jesus is breaking social mores and religious norms. Jesus exorcises a demon from a man on the Sabbath (Luke 4:31–37). He stretches out his hand, touches a leper and heals him (Luke 5:12–16). On another Sabbath day, Jesus heals a man with a withered hand and provokes the ire of the scribes who were watching him (Luke 6:6–11). A woman, who was unclean because of hemorrhaging, touched Jesus's garment and was healed (Luke 8:42–48). Such actions fulfilled the vision of Mary, the mother of Jesus. Her song of praise has come to be called "The Magnificat." In her song, Mary proclaims the greatness of the Lord because:

"He has brought down the powerful from their thrones,
and lifted up the lowly;
he has filled the hungry with good things,
and sent the rich away empty" (Luke 1:52–53).

It was commonly assumed by the Jews that unclean items contaminated the clean. Contact with people who were judged unclean because of their emotional state (evil spirit), their physical condition (leprosy), or physical state and gender (hemorrhaging woman) made a clean person ritually unclean and unable to worship in the temple. Jesus saw things differently.

Jesus understood righteousness to be more powerful than unrighteousness and the light more powerful than the darkness. Rather than the unclean contaminating the clean, Jesus taught that the clean could cleanse the unclean. He demonstrated this truth to his disciples and to those who came to hear him teach and watch him perform miracles. Evil was overcome, the sick were touched, included in the community, and healed. Women were healed and treated as equals.

Halfway through Luke's gospel, Jesus appoints seventy people to go before him and prepare his way. They were instructed to enter the towns,

"Cure the sick who are there, and say to them, 'The kingdom of God has come near to you' " (Luke 10:9). Their ministry was a duplicate of Jesus's ministry. Their ministry was also a prototype for the ministry of the church.

Shortly before he ascended, Luke records Jesus's instructions to the disciples concerning their mission. Jesus says, "But you will receive power when the Holy Spirit has come upon you; and you will be my witnesses in Jerusalem, in all Judea and Samaria, and to the ends of the earth" (Acts 1:8).[1] The ministry that Jesus gave his disciples was to proclaim that God's kingdom of love and grace had arrived. Through the life, death, and resurrection of Jesus, God's kingdom was available to all people.

The gospel of John is significantly different in the way the writer records Jesus's ministry. Yet, like the synoptic gospels—Matthew, Mark, and Luke—the gospel portrays Jesus as the one who brings God's kingdom of love and grace to humankind. That love is demonstrated in Jesus's healing of the sick and the raising of the dead (e.g., John 5:2–9, John 11:17–44). Jesus's ministry goes beyond the Jews and includes Samaritans and Gentiles (John 4:1–26, John 12:20–24). He even reaches out to the needs of a Roman court official and heals the official's sick son, enabling them to encounter God's presence and power as well (John 4:26–50).

During the last week of his life, as recorded in the gospel of John, Jesus gives final instructions to his disciples. The disciples and Jesus come together for what will be Jesus's final meal with them. Before the meal begins, Jesus takes a basin and washes his disciples' feet. This is a menial task that is usually the duty of house slaves. By performing this lowly task, though, Jesus acts out his words that follow. When he is finished washing their feet, Jesus turns to his disciples and says, "I give you a new commandment, that you love one another. Just as I have loved you, you also should love one another" (John 13:34). The disciples and those who followed after them are given the task of loving others in word and deed. This calling is not the reason that God loves them, nor is it the guarantee that God will continue to love them. Rather, it is the response of the disciples and followers of Jesus to God's love and God's gift of salvation. It is also a continuation of Jesus's ministry and a demonstration of life in God's kingdom.

With such a strong, unanimous witness to Jesus's ministry of love and grace, and our call to carry on that ministry, how did the church become so judgmental and so willing to condemn so many people to hell?

---

1. Biblical scholars consider "The Book of Acts" to have been written by the same person that wrote the gospel of Luke.

INROADS OF JUDGMENT—EARLY
WESTERN CHURCH FATHERS

Those first followers of "the Way" bore witness to the coming of the kingdom of God—a kingdom of love and grace. Their egalitarian love feasts may
not have been perfect. Paul corrects the practices of the Corinthian Christians in his first letter to them. Still, all followers of the Way understood that
love was the foundation of their community life. The leaders of the church
reminded them of this constantly. In Peter's first letter to the church, he
encourages his readers to "Above all, maintain constant love for one another,
for love covers a multitude of sins. Be hospitable to one another without
complaining. Like good stewards of the manifold grace of God, serve one
another with whatever gift each of you has received" (1 Pet 4:8–10).

The Corinthian Christians were very religious. They had experienced
an outpouring of the Holy Spirit and demonstrated many of the Spirit's
gifts—speaking in tongues, healing, and prophecy—in their lives together.
Paul warns them, though, that if they do not have love in their relationship
with each other, they have nothing. Paul's words are moving and powerful.
He writes:

> If I speak in the tongues of mortals and of angels, but do not
> have love, I am a noisy gong or a clanging cymbal. And if I have
> prophetic powers, and understand all mysteries and all knowl-
> edge, and if I have all faith, so as to remove mountains, but do
> not have love, I am nothing. If I give away all my possessions,
> and if I hand over my body so that I may boast, but do not have
> love, I gain nothing. Love is patient; love is kind; love is not
> envious or boastful or arrogant or rude. It does not insist on
> its own way; it is not irritable or resentful; it does not rejoice in
> wrongdoing but rejoices in the truth. It bears all things, believes
> all things, hopes all things, endures all things. Love never ends
> (1 Corinthians 13:1–8).

In the letter attributed to James, the author also emphasizes the impor-
tance of love to his readers. In fact, the author clearly states that if a person
claims to have great faith, but doesn't have works of love, the depth or validity of his or her faith is to be questioned. The author observes:

> What good is it, my brothers and sisters, if you say you have faith
> but do not have works? Can faith save you? If a brother or sister
> is naked and lacks daily food, and one of you says to them, "Go
> in peace; keep warm and eat your fill," and yet you do not supply
> their bodily needs, what is the good of that? So faith by itself, if it

has no works, is dead. But someone will say, "You have faith and I have works." Show me your faith apart from your works, and I by my works will show you my faith (James 2:14–18).

Humankind has always had difficulty accepting God's love and grace. The idea that God loves us and there is nothing we can do to increase or decrease God's love for us seems too good to be true. The thought that we can do nothing to earn our salvation—that our salvation is a perfectly free, no-strings-attached gift—confounds us. Such a concept is like the phrase "free lunch." We have been taught that there is no such thing as a free lunch. Somewhere there is a catch or a cost. People have searched the good news of God's love—and fact that we have been reconciled with God because of the life, death, and resurrection of Jesus—looking for a hidden cost. Finding none, they have created a cost—expectations that men and women must meet to be loved and saved.

Thus, the emphasis on love as a theme in the continuation of the ministry of Jesus slowly eroded. By the second century—a little more than one hundred years after the death, resurrection, and ascension of Jesus—the church fathers were proclaiming hell and damnation. Around the year 151 CE, Justin Martyr wrote "No more is it possible for the evildoer, the avaricious, and the treacherous to hide from God than it is for the virtuous. Every man will receive the eternal punishment or reward which his actions deserve. Indeed, if all men recognized this, no one would choose evil even for a short time, knowing that he would incur the eternal sentence of fire. On the contrary, he would take every means to control himself and to adorn himself in virtue, so that he might obtain the good gifts of God and escape the punishments."[2]

Shortly after he makes this proclamation, Justin Martyr announces that there will be a judgment day, at which time the righteous will be rewarded and the unrighteous will suffer eternal punishment. A shift is taking place. The emphasis is now on justice rather than love. Another more important change that is occurring is the focus of the individual Christian's life. No longer are followers of Jesus encouraged to live daily in the reality of God's kingdom of love and grace. Christians are now instructed to live each moment in the shadow of Judgment Day. Justin Martyr writes, "[Jesus] shall come from the heavens in glory with his angelic host, when he shall raise the bodies of all the men who ever lived. Then he will clothe the worthy in immortality; but the wicked, clothed in eternal sensibility, he will commit to the eternal fire, along with the evil demons."[3]

2. Martyr, *The First Apology*, chapter 12.
3. Martyr, *The First Apology*, chapter 52.

As the church moved farther and farther away from Jesus's time on earth, the church also became more distant from Jesus's central message. Other leaders of the church picked up on Justin Martyr's message and echoed it. One of them was Athenagoras, who wrote around 177 CE, "We [Christians] are persuaded that when we are removed from this present life we shall live another life, better than the present one.... Then we shall abide near God and with God, changeless and free from suffering in the soul ... or if we fall with the rest [of mankind], a worse one and in fire; for God has not made us as sheep or beasts of burden, a mere incidental work, that we should perish and be annihilated.[4]

Theological greats such as Tertullian (160–220 CE.), who is considered the Father of the Latin Church, Cyprian (200–258 CE.), a pre-eminent Latin writer of Western Christianity, and Augustine (354–430 CE), one of the church's most prominent theologians, also joined the chorus.[5]

MEDIEVAL CHURCH MESSAGE— DOMINATION THROUGH DAMNATION

In the prologue to the gospel of John, the writer declares, "The light shines in the darkness, and the darkness did not overcome it" (John 1:5). This is true of God's incarnation in the person of Jesus. In the Middle Ages though, the church's emphasis on the doctrine of hell and eternal damnation almost overcame the truth of the light of the kingdom of God's love and grace. Historians have placed the boundaries of the Middle Ages between the Fall of the Western Roman Empire on one end and the beginning of the Renaissance and the Age of Discovery on the other end. This is roughly between the fifth and the fifteenth centuries CE.

Tertullian, Cyprian, and Augustine planted the seeds of fear-based dualism into the teachings of the Western church. Their writings influenced the Western church to such a degree that it "declined into a system of dogmatic hierarchy and spiritual despotism."[6] A battle was taking place between Satan and God. The battlefield was the souls of men and women. Because of humankind's proclivity to sin, the tactical advantage went to Satan. The only hope men and women had for salvation was adherence to those doctrines declared *orthodox* and *truthful* and obedience to church authorities. The good news of God's love, humankind's reconciliation with God through the life, death, and resurrection of Jesus, and the gift of faith were not heard.

4. Athenagoras, *Plea for the Christians*, chapter 31.6.
5. Brazen Church, "Torment Invaded Church Doctrine."
6. Thomson, "Whence Eternity."

Few Christians were literate during the Middle Ages. Even fewer read the works of these three men. The thoughts and ideas of these men, however, were amplified in the church through Jerome's Latin *Vulgate*. Jerome translated this version from unreliable texts in the late fourth century. For over one thousand years, the *Vulgate* was the definitive edition of the most influential text in Western European society.[7] Many words that came to be a part of central church doctrines —such as eternal, redemption, perdition, and damnation—were coined by Tertullian and the others. These words came to be associated with concepts foreign to the original Greek.[8] The tide grew to move the focus of the Christian life from living in God's kingdom to attaining God's kingdom and eternal life and avoiding eternal damnation.

There were some church reformers such as Francis of Assisi (1181– 1226 CE), who attempted to reintroduce the celebration of God's love and grace into the life of the church. "In 1209 [St. Francis] composed a simple rule for his followers ("friars"), the *Regula Primitive* or "Primitive Rule," which came from verses in the Bible. The rule was, 'To follow the teachings of our Lord Jesus Christ and to walk in his footsteps.' "[9] Though St. Francis and others left their mark, their message was drowned out by the raging fires of Hell.

Sickness and death were everywhere in the middle ages. Between 75,000 and 200,000 people died from the "Black Death." The pandemic reached its height between 1347 and 1351. Fifty percent of the children in Europe died before they reached the age of five years. The average life expectancy in the twelfth and thirteenth centuries was 35 years.

> "[With sickness and death so prominent] Death, and the alleviation of its horrors, had been the dominant theme throughout the handbooks of the medieval centuries, and the most sought-after books dwelt on how to escape Hell. Purgatory had been introduced by way of mitigation, the church offering her sacraments and pilgrimages and her indulgences, and the intercession of saints, as a means of relaxing the pressures of Purgatory and reducing its time. Furthermore, the supererogation merits of the saints could allegedly be pooled, with transfer of credits to reduce the purgatorial pains. But while the saved would enjoy an eternity of bliss, the irrevocably damned would suffer everlasting torment, with no mercy of ultimate extinction. The

7. Wikipedia, "Vulgate."

8. Ferwerda, *Raising Hell*, 56.

9. Wikipedia, "Francis of Assisi."

moans of the lost would continue on forever and ever, amid the sulfurous flames."[10]

Instead of comforting its people with the assurance of God's love and presence in their suffering, the Church frightened the people with threats of eternal punishment.

MARTIN LUTHER—GRACE AND FORGIVENESS

Though the Middle Ages were "dark," the light still burned. The fire of God's love and grace was rekindled by the Protestant Reformation, which began in the sixteenth century. Its rallying cry was, "The just shall live by faith." In other words, Christians shall not work hard to get into heaven (and stay out of Hell), but rather live by faith in Christ's gift of salvation and enjoy God's love and grace.

One of the Reformers, Martin Luther, grew up under the influence of the church and its emphasis on condemnation and hell. He struggled with how to please a wrathful and judgmental God and never felt that he was adequate to the task. In his quest to find peace with God, he joined the Augustinian Order. Luther, however, did not find the peace he sought in the basic living conditions, course robes, fasting, prayer, and self-flagellations of monastic life.

Luther was sent by the Augustinian Order to become a Biblical scholar and, eventually, Luther earned a doctorate in sacred studies. It was in his study of the scripture that he encountered Paul's radical understanding of God's grace for humankind. Paul writes in his letter to the Ephesians, "For by grace you have been saved through faith, and this is not your own doing; it is the gift of God— not the result of works, so that no one may boast. For we are what he has made us, created in Christ Jesus for good works, which God prepared beforehand to be our way of life" (Eph 2:8–10). The light dawned for Luther. He realized that he was incapable of pleasing God through his works, and he didn't need to. It was through Jesus's life, death, and resurrection that he, and all humankind, were able to experience God's grace.

Luther's recaptured understanding of God's grace led him to question many of the church's practices of his day. He nailed ninety-five discussion points, or theses, to the church's door at Wittenberg on October 31, 1517. This action is often cited as the beginning of the Protestant Reformation.

Martin Luther didn't dwell on humankind's condemnation and hell. He stressed the preaching of the gospel rather than the law. The focus of the

10. Froom, *The Conditionalist Faith*, chapter 4.

gospel was on what God had done through the life, death, and resurrection of Jesus—to reconcile and save humankind. The law was the opposite of the gospel. The law focused on what men and women thought they had to do to earn God's love and be saved. Luther would say that the gospel leads to life, while the law leads to death. He wanted people to rejoice in God's gift and to live in its reality. To live under the burden of the law and the threat of condemnation and hell was not the message of the cross of Christ.

Another reason that Luther did not emphasize God's condemnation and hell is that he did not believe in the immortality of the soul. During its two-thousand-year history, two views of the afterlife have woven their ways through the teachings of the church. The concept that part of a human being—the soul—is immortal and never dies is based on Greek philosophy. Greek philosophers such as Plato taught that two parts, the body and the soul (or spirit), make up the human being. When a person dies, the mortal, perishable body disintegrates and returns to dust. The immortal soul, at death, is freed from the body and soars either to the perfection of heaven or plummets to the realm of hell.

The concept of the immortal soul fit perfectly into the church's teaching on purgatory, heaven, and hell. Church leaders taught that at death the body and soul of the believer separated. The body was buried or burned, while the individual believer's soul entered purgatory. In purgatory, the soul worked off the judgment of its accumulated sins until it could, in the future, enter heaven. Those who died outside of the church—the unbaptized—immediately went to Hell, where they were condemned to their eternal punishment.

There is almost no Biblical backing to the idea of the immortality of the soul. Supporters of this teaching frequently cite as a proof text the conversation between Jesus and one of the convicts who was crucified with him. The condemned man believes that Jesus is innocent and has caught a glimpse of Jesus as the Messiah. The man asks Jesus to remember him when Jesus comes into his kingdom. Jesus replies, "Truly I tell you, today you will be with me in Paradise" (Luke 23:43). The words *today* and *in Paradise* are understood by those who believe in the immortality of the soul as irrefutable evidence their belief is the truth.

There is, of course, another way to interpret this passage of Scripture. Many Biblical scholars and theologians place the emphasis of Jesus's comment on the words *with me*. They believe that Jesus is speaking words of comfort and encouragement to the condemned man. Jesus is telling him that death will not be able to separate the man from God. The man will always be with Jesus. Support for such an idea is found in Matthew's gospel, "And remember, I am with you always, to the end of the age" (Matt 28:20), and in Paul's words to the Romans, "For I am convinced that neither death, nor life, nor angels, nor rulers, nor things present, nor things to come, nor powers, nor height, nor depth, nor anything else in all creation, will be able to separate us from the love of God in Christ Jesus our Lord" (Rom 8:38–39).

The second view of the afterlife has its roots in the teachings of Jewish Rabbis. They rejected the idea that human beings are made up of two parts. They viewed the body and soul as one and did not believe that it could be divided in any way. When a person died there was no separation. The body decayed and the soul slept. Both awaited the resurrection at the end of time. Paul communicates this idea to the Christians in Thessalonica when he writes, "But we do not want you to be uninformed, brothers, about those who are asleep, that you may not grieve as others do who have no hope. For since we believe that Jesus died and rose again, even so, through Jesus, God will bring with him those who have fallen asleep" (1 Thess 4:13–14 ESV). Paul again stresses the idea of sleep of death and the hope of the resurrection in his letter to the church in Corinth. He writes, "And if Christ has not been raised, your faith is futile and you are still in your sins. Then those also who have fallen asleep in Christ have perished. If in Christ we have hope in this life only, we are of all people most to be pitied. But in fact, Christ has been raised from the dead, the firstfruits of those who have fallen asleep" (1 Cor 15:17–20 ESV).

As a Biblical scholar and teacher, Luther worked from the perspective that at death the person entered into the sleep of death. The idea of the immortal soul suffering through purgatory after death does not fit into view, nor does it coincide with Luther's understanding of the gospel and what Jesus accomplished through his life, death, and resurrection. In this view of death, the sleep of believers continues until the coming of Jesus. It is at that time that they shall be awakened and resurrected. It is also at that time that they shall stand before the throne of God.[11]

Though Luther placed a great emphasis on God's grace through the life, death, and resurrection of Jesus, he did not let loose the doctrine of hell. Luther envisioned believers standing before the judgment throne of God and being declared righteous because of Jesus's work. Unbelievers would be condemned to Hell, however. Their punishment would be eternal.[12]

11. Froom, *The Conditionalist Faith*, chapter 4.
12. Froom, *The Conditionalist Faith*, chapter 4.

JOHN CALVIN—TOTAL DEPRAVITY
AND PREDESTINATION

Other reformers had a more robust concept of hell. John Calvin, another of the leaders of the Reformation, not only carried on the church's traditional understanding of hell, but he also amplified it. He writes:

> As language cannot describe the severity of the divine vengeance on the reprobate, their pains and torments are figured to us by corporeal things, such as darkness, wailing and gnashing of teeth, inextinguishable fire, the ever-gnawing worm (Matthew 8:12; 22:13; Mark 9:43; Isaiah 66:24). It is certain that by such modes of expression the Holy Spirit designed to impress all our senses with dread, as when it is said, "Tophet is ordained of old; yea, for the king it is prepared: he has made it deep and large; the pile thereof is fire and much wood; the breath of the Lord, like a stream of brimstone, does kindle it" (Isaiah 30:33). As we thus require to be assisted to conceive the miserable doom of the reprobate, so the consideration on which we ought chiefly to dwell is the fearful consequence of being estranged from all fellowship with God, and not only so, but of feeling that His majesty is adverse to us, while we cannot possibly escape from it.[13]

Calvin's horrendous understanding of hell and his emphasis on it is made even more deplorable by his declaration that men and women are predestined to hell by God. One of the five main points of Calvinism is "Unconditional Election." This teaching states, "God does not base His election on anything He sees in the individual. He chooses the elect according to the kind intention of His will (Eph. 1:4–8; Rom. 9:11) without any consideration of merit within the individual. Nor does God look into the future to see who would pick Him. Also, as some are elected into salvation, others are not" (Rom. 9:15, 21).[14]

God is in control of the destiny of people. Some people will enjoy the benefits of heaven, while others (Native Americans, pagans, and infidels, etc.) will suffer eternally. The light shines and the darkness cannot extinguish it. Still, the darkness at this time in history is a powerful force. The shout of the lies drowns out the whisper of the truth.

---

13. Calvin, *Institutes*, book 3, chapter 25, section 12.
14. Calvinist Corner, "Five Points."

THE GREAT AWAKENING—SINNERS IN
THE HANDS OF AN ANGRY GOD

The struggle between light and darkness, truth and lies, continued in history as it still does today. An example can be seen in eighteenth-century Americana. Two hundred years after the start of the Reformation, a religious movement called the First Great Awakening (1730–1740) spread across the colonies. In this movement, hell was effectively used to incite the masses and convince them to give their lives to Jesus.

Jonathan Edwards was one of the prominent preachers in this religious revival. Edwards was born with religion in his blood, His father was a minister, as was his maternal grandfather. After completing his studies at Yale University, Edwards became a Congregationalist pastor.[15]

The goal of Edwards and other revivalist preachers of the First Great Awakening was "To [make] religion intensely personal to the average person by fostering a deep sense of spiritual conviction of personal sin and need for redemption, and by encouraging introspection and a commitment to a new standard of personal morality."[16] Hell and the threat of eternal damnation was their tool to accomplish this task.

Edwards's use of hell to achieve his purposes can be seen clearly in his classic sermon, "Sinners in the Hands of an Angry God." In that sermon he preaches:

> The God that holds you over the pit of hell, much as one holds a spider, or some loathsome insect over the fire, abhors you, and is dreadfully provoked: his wrath towards you burns like fire; he looks upon you as worthy of nothing else, but to be cast into the fire; he is of purer eyes than to bear to have you in his sight; you are ten thousand times more abominable in his eyes, than the most hateful venomous serpent is in ours. You have offended him infinitely more than ever a stubborn rebel did his prince; and yet it is nothing but his hand that holds you from falling into the fire every moment. It is to be ascribed to nothing else, that you did not go to hell the last night; that you was suffered to awake again in this world, after you closed your eyes to sleep. And there is no other reason to be given, why you have not dropped into hell since you arose in the morning, but that God's hand has held you up. There is no other reason to be given why you have not gone to hell, since you have sat here in the house of God, provoking his pure eyes by your sinful wicked manner

15. Wikipedia, "The Great Awakening."
16. Wikipedia, "The Great Awakening."

of attending his solemn worship. Yea, there is nothing else that is to be given as a reason why you do not this very moment drop down into hell.

O sinner! Consider the fearful danger you are in: it is a great furnace of wrath, a wide and bottomless pit, full of the fire of wrath, that you are held over in the hand of that God, whose wrath is provoked and incensed as much against you, as against many of the damned in hell. You hang by a slender thread, with the flames of divine wrath flashing about it, and ready every moment to singe it, and burn it asunder; and you have no interest in any Mediator, and nothing to lay hold of to save yourself, nothing to keep off the flames of wrath, nothing of your own, nothing that you ever have done, nothing that you can do, to induce God to spare you one moment.[17]

Revivalist preachers like Dwight L. Moody, Billy Sunday, and even Billy Graham have continued to emphasize the threat of hell in their preaching. Dwight L. Moody held revival meetings during the mid-nineteenth century. In one of his sermons he proclaimed:

Tonight you may be saved. We are trying to win you to Christ, and if you go down from this building to hell you will remember the meetings we had here. You will remember how these ministers looked, how the people looked, and how it has seemed sometimes as if we were in the very presence of God himself. In that lost world you won't hear that beautiful hymn, "Jesus of Nazareth Passeth By." He will have passed by. There will be no Jesus passing that way. There will be no sweet songs of Zion there. No little children either to pray for their impenitent fathers and mothers.[18]

In the early twentieth century, Billy Sunday was the best-known revivalist preacher. He is quoted as saying, "Hell is the highest reward that the devil can offer you for being a servant of his."[19] Billy Graham writes, "Down inside we all yearn to live forever. It's the reason why people spend enormous amounts of time and money trying to keep old age at bay. But death is a reality, and beyond it is eternity —either with God in Heaven, or in that place of absolute despair the Bible calls Hell. Don't gamble with your soul, but put your faith and trust in Christ for your salvation today."[20]

17. Edwards, "Sinners in the Hands."
18. Moody, "Jesus is Savior."
19. Sunday, "Quotes."
20. Graham, "Don't Gamble."

Do you see the shift, which has taken place over the centuries? We have heard the lie so often that we now believe it to be the truth. When Jesus walked beside the Sea of Galilee, he met Peter and his brother, Andrew. Jesus' invitation to them was to, "Follow me, and I will make you fish for people" (Matthew 4:19). Jesus was inviting the two men to live in a relationship with God and to experience God's love and grace. This is to live in God's kingdom. Their lives would be changed forever along with their purpose for living. No longer would they live simply to put food on their tables. Now, they would live to serve and to carry on Jesus's ministry, when the time came. In Jesus's words, there was no threat of God's wrath and eternal condemnation. The emphasis was on living every day in God's kingdom.

For almost two millennia the church has preached and taught about the existence of hell rather than to proclaim the gospel message. The idea of hell is deeply engrained in the minds of most Christians. Today hell is still used to control those who identify themselves as believers in Jesus Christ and to condemn those outside the fold of the church.

HELL TODAY—STORIES OF JUDGMENT AND SEPARATION

Like a man going to the gallows, fourteen-year-old Skylar[21] thumped down the stairs. His head hung down and his shoulders slumped. He knew his world, as he had known it, was coming to an end. His family's façade of a loving, Christian household, with no flaws, was going to be shattered. He could see no signs of hope; no light on the horizon. There was only condemnation and darkness.

Earlier in the day, Skylar's mother had barged into his room at an inopportune time. She had caught Skylar and a neighborhood friend in a compromising situation. Shocked, Skylar's mother had ordered the other boy to get dressed and to get out of their house immediately. With barely controlled rage, she had commanded Skylar to stay in his room until his father came home.

Skylar's father had come home about ten minutes ago. He could hear his father and mother talking from his room. They were not quiet. Their voices rose in pitch and in anger. They had yelled from the bottom of the stairs for him to come down immediately. With no other option, Skylar obeyed.

---

21. Names used in this book, unless otherwise noted, are fictitious. The stories are compilations of several accounts.

Shuffling into the kitchen, Skylar glanced at his father. The man's face was red. His eyes were filled with hate and his mouth fixed in a sneer. He pointed to a chair between him and his wife. "Sit down," he growled.

Skylar did not dare to look at his mother. He sat down with arms on his knees staring at the floor.

His father bent down, grabbed Skylar by the hair, forcing Skylar to look at him and yelled, "Is it true?"

Skylar was silent.

"Answer me," his father commanded. "Were you having sex with another boy?"

Skylar swallowed. Trying to avoid his father's eyes, he whispered, "Yes."

"Are you a faggot?" his father hissed.

Skylar said nothing.

"Did you hear me? I asked you a question. Are you a faggot?"

The word grated on him like "nigger" would have if he were black or "bitch" if he were a woman. Yet his father—the good Christian man that he was—would never understand that. Those words were not politically correct—it wasn't "Christian" to use them—but using the word "faggot" was okay. It was okay because faggots were cursed by God. People who engaged in same-sex relations were deplorable. They were unnatural and what they did was sinful—it said so in the Bible.

His father was wrong, Skylar thought. The man might be his father, but he was wrong on this subject—and probably several others. Skylar decided, as he sat in the chair under his parents' glowering stares, that he would not let them intimidate him. Like it or not, he knew who and what he was.

Skylar straightened up and brought his shoulders back. His father dropped the hold that he had on Skylar's hair. Skylar turned and looked at his mother and turned back and looked into his father's eyes. He took a deep breath. "I am gay." He said it as a proclamation.

His father turned away in disgust.

"When did you decide to be gay?" his mother asked.

With gathering resolve, Skylar replied, "I never decided to be gay. It is not a decision that you make, it is who you discover yourself to be."

"That's not what Pastor Bennett says." His mother shot back.

"As far as I know, Pastor Bennett isn't gay, so how would he know?"

Spinning around, Skylar's father threatened, "Don't get sassy with your mother."

Skylar looked down at the floor momentarily and shuffled his feet. He then looked up at his father. "I don't mean to be sassy," he replied apologetically. "I only wanted to say that I am gay and that is not a decision on my part. I am simply telling you who I am."

"Well, you're going to have to change," his mother declared. "If you continue in this sinful behavior, you'll be condemned to eternal punishment. You'll go to Hell." Her lip quivered ever so slightly. Her eyes became watery. "I certainly don't want my son to go to Hell." Skylar's mother quickly turned away and wiped her eyes.

"I've sat through enough of Pastor Bennett's sermons to know what he thinks the Bible says about gays. I don't think he's right. I've thought a lot about this. I've known I'm gay since I was eleven. I didn't tell you because I knew that something like this would happen. I've prayed about this and thought about this for three years. I am who I am, and God made me who I am. If God made me gay, then I can't imagine that God would condemn me or anyone like me to hell. It just doesn't make sense, and it isn't what a loving God would do."

"Hmm," his father grunted. "I'm certainly impressed at fourteen you think you know as much about the Bible and God as Pastor Bennett, who has gone to college and seminary and even has a doctorate." He shook his head. "I don't know if you're going to hell or not, though that's where I think people like you should go. One thing I do know is that you will not be living in my house. I refuse to live with a faggot in my house, even if he is my son. I'm calling my brother, Sid, to see if he'd put up with you and your kind."

Skylar's father waved his hand toward the stairs. "Until you leave, you're confined to your room. I suggest you begin to pack. I don't want to see your face again. You are no son of mine."

Mary Beth is a forty-five-year-old entrepreneur. She and her husband, Carl, own their own fabrication company. It is very successful. In addition to growing a business, which employs scores of people and provides a tidy income, the two of them have raised three children. Their oldest is a sophomore in college and the other two are in high school—a junior and a freshman. They are all strong students and fair athletes and appear to be well-adjusted teenagers. They're good kids. Certainly, Mary Beth and Carl have had their troubles and have experienced hard times. On the whole, however, they are living the good life and are thankful for their many blessings.

That's not good enough for Mary Beth's mother, Madge, though. She is constantly trying to coax Mary Beth to attend church services. Mary Beth hasn't been to church since she left for college over twenty-five years ago. Madge wants more than regular church attendance from Mary Beth and her family. Madge wants them to accept Jesus Christ as their Lord and Savior. Until they do that, it is her firm belief that Mary Beth and family are doomed to an eternal punishment in hell. A recent conversation the two women had over coffee and Danish exemplified this.

Madge started the conversation by relating how she had appreciated the latest preaching series at her congregation. The pastor had entitled the series, "Discipleship Today." "I was impressed," Madge shared, "with the emphasis that Pastor Paul placed on taking a stand, identifying with Jesus, and living out your faith." He based the series on a verse in Paul's letter to the Romans, "If you openly declare that Jesus is Lord and believe in your heart that God raised him from the dead, you will be saved" (Rom 10:9).

"Mmhmm," Mary Beth hummed and nodded her head to indicate that she was listening. "Don't you just love this Danish?" Mary Beth said to change the subject. "It's flavorful, flaky, and so light. It just melts in your mouth."

"It's good but not as good as Pastor Paul's sermon," Madge shot back, deflecting Mary Beth's effort to sidetrack the conversation. "He really stressed how important it was for us to take a stand, not only for our sake but also for the sake of the world."

"Yes, Mom, I understand. I've heard it all before."

"Have you? Have you really heard that before? If you have, then why haven't you acted on it? Why haven't you given your life to Jesus and come back to church?"

"I haven't done that because I refuse to believe in a god who would condemn a majority of the world's population to eternal punishment and hell. Such a god is not a loving god and he, she, or it is not a god that I want to worship or have as a part of my life."

Madge shook her head. "I just don't understand what happened to turn you against the Lord."

"You don't? I can tell you the exact time. I was sixteen and my best friend in all of the world was Sylvia—Sylvia Weisman. Sylvia was a Jew. One night you mentioned how sad it was that Sylvia was a Jew because it meant that she was going to hell. I asked you why you would believe such an awful thing and you quoted a Bible verse. Somewhere in the Bible, you said that Jesus taught his disciples that he was "the way, the truth and the life and that no one could come to the father except through him."

"Yes. That's John 14:6," Madge agreed.

"That's what did it for me. I couldn't imagine why a god would condemn a wonderful person like Sylvia to hell just because she was Jewish. I then began to think of other friends of mine. Curt never went to church. He said he was an atheist. Curt was a sweet, considerate, and loving guy. I couldn't have asked for a better guy friend. According to your god, though, he was doomed to unimaginable agony for eternity because he didn't know Jesus."

"That was just the tip of the iceberg, so to speak. There are all those people—millions and millions of them—all around the world who have never heard about Jesus. None of them believe the way you think they are supposed to believe. All of them condemned to hell. What kind of a loving god would do that? Certainly not one in which I would want to believe."

"Now, you can continue to talk about your god of love who condemns everyone to hell. I'll leave and you can drink your coffee alone. Or we can change the subject and enjoy our coffee and Danish together. It's your decision."

2

Changing Theology

Our Understanding of God is Dynamic

Before we shine a more intensive light on the origins and development of the doctrines of hell and eternal damnation, we must reflect on the nature of theology. Heraclitus, a sixth-century BCE Greek philosopher, is noted for observing that the only constant in life is change. We may be uncomfortable admitting it, but this is true even of our theological beliefs.

As we journey through life, our understanding of the world around us and our beliefs about God change. We go from an unquestioning, childish, Sunday school faith to a deeper faith. Paul said it best when he wrote, "When I was a child, I spoke like a child, I thought like a child, I reasoned like a child; when I became an adult, I put an end to childish ways" (1 Cor. 13:11). Paul is not saying his faith became watered down, or that he suddenly gave up temple worship. That didn't happen with Paul and it usually doesn't happen to our faith, either. Rather, we move from a bland, Gerber pureed peas type of faith to a faith that is a delicious, slow-roasted prime rib encrusted with fresh herbs and pepper, hand-carved and served with homemade au jus and creamy horseradish sauce.

HOLIDAY STORIES AND CUSTOMS—
MISCELLANEOUS ADDITIONS

It wasn't too shocking when we learned that Easter baskets, chocolate bunnies, and colored eggs had absolutely nothing to do with the Easter story and the proclamation of Jesus's resurrection. As children, the important point for us was that we found our Easter basket and received our Easter treats. It was a little disappointing to discover it was really our parents who hid the colorful eggs and overflowing baskets. Our childhood beliefs, though, were sacrificed on the altar of growing up and replaced by other parts of our Easter celebrations.

Realizing that there wasn't a Santa Claus who delivered all of the Christmas presents to all the girls and boys in the entire world was a little more difficult. The blow of *knowing* the truth about Santa Claus was not softened by the many Christmas movies featuring the jolly old man. Not even the 1897 "Yes, Virginia, There Is a Santa Claus," letter helped take away the disappointment we felt.

Later on, we discovered that Jesus wasn't born on December 25, 0000. This was a little more traumatic. The pastor tried to soften the blow by telling us that nobody really knew when Jesus was born; they could only guess. Pope Julius was the one who officially designated December 25th as the celebration of Jesus's birth. He did this around 340 CE. He purposely placed it on a date when pagans were celebrating the winter solstice. Chronological hints in the Bible had little or nothing to do with his choice of the date.[1]

As we grow, mature, and experience more of life, our perspective on life changes. We let go of things we once thought to be true. These are replaced by new knowledge, deeper understanding, and a broader perspective of life. To cling to our childhood as we age into the various stages of adulthood is usually not healthy nor helpful.

CHANGING PERCEPTIONS OF GOD—
FROM WRATH TO LOVE

Before we go much further in our discussion on theology, hell, and eternal damnation, we need to affirm two things. First, that god is god and doesn't change. The writer to the letter to the Hebrews asserts, "Jesus Christ is the same yesterday and today and forever" (Heb. 13:8). God doesn't change, but our comprehension and opinion of God does. This happens in each of our relationships, and not just the relationship that we have with God.

1. Why Christmas, "Christmas Customs."

Remember when we were teenagers? We thought our parents were not "cool" and dumb. We knew so much more than they did. We were so wise. After a few years, when we were in our mid-twenties or early thirties, we suddenly realized how smart and wise our parents really were (and how dumb and immature *we* were). All of us have had the experience where we considered someone to be our close, personal friend. When the chips were down, though, they betrayed us. Our opinion of them quickly changed and our relationship with them was altered.

Many people, when they read the Hebrew Scriptures, begin to see God as a God of wrath and judgment. It is easy to do. After all, God wiped out almost every living thing on earth, according to Genesis 6–7, because of humankind's wickedness. The Israelites believed that they endured countless invasions and plundering in the period of the Judges because of their unfaithfulness to God. They would repent and plead with God to send help. God, hearing their prayer, would send a charismatic leader, who was called a judge, to lead them in victory over their enemies. Many times, God appeared merciless in God's judgment against enemies of the Israelites. When King Saul attacked the Amalekites, God instructed him to kill man and woman, child and infant, ox and sheep, camel and donkey (1 Sam 15:3). The Northern Kingdom's defeat by the Assyrians and the Southern Kingdom's exile to Babylon were understood to be God's judgment upon God's people for their faithlessness and their devotion to other gods. With all of the killing and destruction, it is easy to get the impression that God is a deity that a person should not anger. This perspective of God has largely gone by the wayside, though a few pastors and Christian leaders continue to have it. According to many Christians, God's judgment was avowed upon the LGBTQ community and drug addicts with the AIDS pandemic of the 1980s and 1990s. When hurricane Katrina devastated New Orleans, several Christian personalities declared that Katrina was God's judgment upon the city because of its sinfulness. We occasionally catch ourselves asking the question, "What have I done to deserve this?" This may mark a time of self-reflection. It can also be a time when we think that God is punishing us for something, but we're not quite sure what it is.

Students of the Bible not only see God's judgment in the stories of the Hebrew Scriptures but also demonstrations of God's love. From the flood to the Babylonian Captivity, God's actions can be seen as inspired and motivated by love. God was always moving to bring God's people back into a relationship with God. God was not content to let God's people wander. The Lord moved to declare God's love for the people and to draw them back into a dynamic, living relationship. The Psalmist declares this truth in Psalm 136. In this Psalm, the worship leader recites the account of creation and the history of Israel. The congregation's refrain in this song of worship is, "His steadfast love endures forever."

God, as a God of love, is most clearly seen in the person of Jesus. Certainly, Jesus had issues with the pompous religiosity of the Pharisees and the corruption that had seeped into the institution of the Temple. The emphasis of Jesus's ministry, though, was on God's steadfast love, overwhelming grace, and unconditional forgiveness. Jesus cured the sick, cleansed lepers, exorcised demons, spoke to and healed women, and even ministered to the needs of the Gentiles. Jesus, by his life, death, and resurrection, enabled us to see the person of God in a different light. God didn't change, but our understanding of who God is and our perspective on the many facets of God's being was altered.

ACCEPTING THE GENTILES—A SEISMIC CHANGE

Our second affirmation is that the Bible is inspired and authoritative. (This is *not* to say that it is infallible or inerrant.) In other words, we believe that God is speaking to us through the words of the Bible. These words are intended to have an impact on our lives and influence our journeys of faith. Like our comprehension and opinions of God, though, our understanding of God's word changes.

This can be clearly seen in the early church's struggle with Gentile Christians. Jesus was a Jew. His disciples and early followers were all Jews. A fundamental principle of the Jewish faith, at that time, was that Jews were to be separate from Gentiles. Association with Gentiles was forbidden; to come in contact with Gentiles made a Jew unclean and unable to worship at the Temple until the individual had been purified. This need for the Jews to keep separate from the surrounding nations was emphasized many times throughout the Hebrew Scriptures. The Jewish Christians' insistence that Gentiles needed to first become Jews before they could become Christians was solidly based on their understanding of the teaching of Scripture. Attitudes and perspectives changed, though, through the movement of the Holy Spirit.

The story of this change is found in Acts 10. Peter was visiting Simon the Tanner in Joppa. Peter became drowsy and decided to take a nap. During his slumber, Peter had a vision where all sorts of animals were lowered in a sheet. God commanded Peter to take and eat from the smorgasbord, which was presented before him, but Peter refused to do so. For Peter to obey would break kosher laws. The vision occurred three times so that Peter would understand that it came from God rather than an upset stomach.

At the same time, a Roman centurion by the name of Cornelius had a vision. The vision instructed him to send members of his household to Peter in Joppa and ask him to come to Cornelius in Caesarea. Cornelius obeyed the vision. Peter accepted the invitation and, when Peter arrived at Cornelius' home, he began to understand what the Holy Spirit was doing—changing the Spirit's interpretation of Scripture. Peter began his impromptu sermon by saying, "I truly understand that God shows no partiality, but in every nation anyone who fears him and does what is right is acceptable to him" (Acts 10:34–35). In the middle of his sermon, the Holy Spirit interrupted Peter and confirmed Peter's new perspective. The Holy Spirit, "fell upon all who heard the word. The circumcised believers who had come with Peter were astounded that the gift of the Holy Spirit had been poured out even on the Gentiles, for they heard them speaking in tongues and extolling God" (Acts 10:44–46).

This reinterpretation of Scripture was a watershed event. It involved a total overhaul of the Jewish world view. Before, the world had been neatly divided into two groups—Jews and Gentiles; those who were God's people and those who were not God's people. In one swoop, the Holy Spirit expanded God's family to include the whole world. God's family was comprised of everyone who feared God and did what was right.

Through the centuries, our understanding of the Bible has continued to evolve. Copernicus and Galileo pointed out to the church authorities that the solar system was heliocentric and not geocentric. The church put up quite a fuss, quoting several passages of Scripture that were felt to support the idea that the sun revolved around the earth and not vice versa. Science prevailed, though, and now most Christians accept the idea that the solar system is heliocentric.

As the centuries passed, the church altered its focus. Instead of lifting up God's gift of salvation as an expression of God's love and grace, the church professed good works for pleasing God. The expectations for good works became so high that only a few people, who were designated as "saints," accumulated enough good works to attain salvation. The Protestant Reformation recaptured the truth of salvation by grace through faith and allowed Christians to see the purpose of good works in an entirely different light.

SLAVERY—SEGREGATION TO CIVIL RIGHTS

In the eighteenth and early nineteenth centuries, chattel slavery was common in the United States. The Bible included several references to enslaved people from Abraham to the time of Paul and the early church. When the practice of slavery was beginning to be questioned, these passages were used to support the institution. The line of reasoning was, "if it was good enough for the people in the Bible, it should be good enough for us." The story of the curse of Noah's son, Ham (Gen. 9:20–28), was interpreted in such a way that the capture, importation, and enslavement of African men and women were justified.

Many people began to interpret the Scripture differently. They understood the Bible to affirm the worth of every individual. All of creation was the Lord's. This included every man, woman, and child. All of humankind were God's children and no one was meant to be the property of another. God's command that God's followers were called to love their neighbor as themselves and the practice of slavery were deemed incompatible.

The tide of human opinion turned against an interpretation of Scripture that supported slavery. Scripture didn't change, but our interpretation of its teachings did. In some countries, like England, slavery ended by an act of Parliament in 1833. In the United States, it took the horrendous struggle of the Civil War to end slavery—and forcibly changed the way we understood the message of the Bible.

A century later, a segregated nation was challenged to reinterpret its understanding of the Bible's teachings. White Christians used the Bible to support their treatment of African Americans in a subhuman fashion. The KKK was generally made up of "good" Christian churchmen, who believed themselves to be justified in lynching Black men and boys. Unequal education systems were seen as supported by Scripture. African Americans may have no longer been enslaved, but they were deemed subservient by a dominant white culture.

Things began to change when Rosa Parks decided, after a long, hard day, not to give up her bus seat to a white person. The practices of Christians and their understanding of the Bible were challenged by Supreme Court decisions, government legislation, and civil disobedience. Though racism is still a reality in the United States and "Christian" white supremacist groups still claim Biblical validation, a majority of Christians understand that the Bible teaches that we are all God's children and we are all equal in God's sight (and should be treated equally in this life on earth).

MEN AND WOMEN IN THE CHURCH—FROM MALE DOMINATION TO SHARED LEADERSHIP

Changes continue. Since the 1960s and 1970s, men's domination of the church has been questioned. Again, a few verses of scripture are quoted to justify the practice of keeping women out of leadership positions in the church. Several denominations now allow women to assume leadership positions and even become ordained. Unfortunately, this is still a minority in the worldwide church, but the change is spreading.

Most recently, the church is being challenged to reassess its understanding of the Queer Community. For centuries the church has promoted the persecution, torture, and even killing of people who identify themselves as LGBTQ. The attitude and actions of the church were based on fourteen passages of Scripture. Many people in many parts of the Christian church are abandoning these archaic teachings of the church and are accepting members of the Queer Community for who they are—God's people. The fourteen passages in Scripture, which previously have been used to support homophobia and the persecution of the Queer Community, have not been forgotten nor ignored. Biblical scholars, though, now have a clearer comprehension of the context in which these verses were written and the purpose for which they were inscribed. With a better understanding of these Scripture texts, our interpretation has been changed and the application of these verses altered.

To be invited to view the Bible from a different perspective is not a call to reject the teachings of Scripture. Neither is it an evil trick to draw us away from the truth. Such an invitation is an encouragement to open our hearts and our heads and discern whether or not the Holy Spirit may be leading us to a new understanding of God's Word and a fresh perspective on life and the world in which we live.

3

A History of Hell

A Non-Biblical Church Doctrine

SHEOL AND GEHENNA—NOT SYNONYMOUS WITH HELL

With the invitation to explore new possibilities and perspectives fresh in our minds, let's delve into the doctrine of hell and eternal damnation. Again, this is not a journey to abandon the truth. Rather, it is an examination of the facts to develop a clearer understanding of the topic and perhaps to move closer to the truth.

One of the greatest surprises, when we begin to study the doctrine of hell, is that hell is not a Biblical concept. In the original languages of the Hebrew Bible and the New Testament, there is no word hell. Other words such as Sheol, Gehenna, and Tartarus have been translated as hell when converted into the English language.

In the Hebrew Scriptures, the place of the dead is named "Sheol." The word literally means, "Unseen."[1] Sheol is the concept that people of ancient times developed to describe the afterlife experience, of which they had no knowledge.[2] In Psalm 88, the Psalmist was tormented and believed he was near death. He wrote, "For my soul is full of troubles, and my life draws near

1. McMillen, "A Biblical Staple."
2. Ferwerda, *Raising Hell*, 40.

31

to Sheol" (Ps 88:3). Again, in Psalm 18: 5 the Psalmist faced the prospect of death. He penned these words, "The cords of Sheol entangled me; the snares of death confronted me." It is obvious that Sheol is not a place to which the Psalmist looked forward. It is not a place of comfort or celebration. The writer of Ecclesiastes painted a rather gloomy picture of Sheol, when he wrote, "Whatever your hand finds to do, do with your might; for there is no work or thought or knowledge or wisdom in Sheol, to which you are going" (Eccl 9:10). Still, a person is not separated from God in Sheol. Reflecting on the presence of God in his life, the Psalmist wrote, "If I ascend to heaven, you are there; if I make my bed in Sheol, you are there" (Ps 139:8). There is nothing attractive about Sheol. It doesn't have fluffy white clouds, streets paved with gold, and humungous banquets with endless food. Neither does it have eternal fires. In the Hebrew Scripture, Sheol is never portrayed as a place of judgment and punishment.

The transformation of Sheol to Hades and finally to Hell began with the Septuagint.[3] The Jews had scattered around the Mediterranean Sea. Lacking the proximity to the Temple and frequent exposure to Hebrew, the dispersed Jews began to lose contact with the words of Scripture. Instead, they were immersed in the prominent Greek culture. At the same time, Greek became a more popular language, so that most of the people in Israel spoke Greek as their primary language. To counteract this dire situation, it was decided to translate the Hebrew Scriptures into Greek. This took place in the third and second centuries BCE. Legend has it that seventy scholars took part in the translation. The word, "Septuagint" comes from the Latin word for "seventy."[4]

Looking for a Greek word they could use to translate the word, "Sheol," the seventy scholars chose "Hades." "In Hellenistic literature the word *"hades"* was used to mean a variety of things: a grave or tomb; the domain of the dead; the dead, collectively (e.g., one's ancestors or forefathers); or what it had originally meant, the place where dead spirits end up after dying."[5] In many ways, Hades was a good translation of the word, Sheol. In later centuries, under the influence of Greek philosophy, though, the word Hades would be transformed. It would become a place of eternal judgment.

Just as Sheol was translated Hades in the Septuagint translation of the Hebrew Scriptures, so the Aramaic word "Gehenna" was translated as Hell in the New Testament. There are twelve times that Gehenna is mentioned in the New Testament, and each of these instances the word is translated

---

3. Early Christian History, "The Theology of Hell."

4. Got Questions, "The Septuagint."

5. Early Christian History, "The Theology of Hell."

Hell. Gehenna is the only word that Jesus used when he alluded to a place of judgment. Another word which is translated as Hell is the word "Tartarus." It is used once and can be found in 2 Pet 2:4. Tartarus, in Greek mythology, is a place of torment and is located under Hades.[6] In Peter's letter, the word is used in reference to the judgment of fallen angels.

Gehenna was a well-known location throughout Israel. It was a place of evil where sacrifices to various foreign gods and idols were carried out. Child sacrifices to the god Molech are mentioned taking place in Gehenna, in 2 Chronicles 28:3. King Josiah, who reigned from 640 to 609 BCE, was a reformer king. He sought to return the People of Israel to the worship of the one true God, Yahweh. As part of his reformation endeavors, he desecrated Topheth, which was located in the Valley of Hinnom (Gehenna) so that sacrifices, especially the sacrifices of children, could no longer take place there (2 Kings 23:10).[7] The valley continued to be used as a place to discard and burn idol artifacts as part of Josiah's purge.[8] Later the valley became a sewage dump. It was a place where dead bodies were thrown whenever proper burials could not be provided for them. Gehenna was a place of decay, stench, and smoldering fires. When Jesus refers to Gehenna as "where their worm does not die, and the fire is not quenched" (Mark 9:43–48) he is making a clear connection to the valley's historic past, using the language of Isaiah 66.[9] Jesus is not referring to a place of eternal condemnation and suffering.

GREEK INFLUENCE—RELIGIOUS, MYTHIC, AND PHILOSOPHICAL

Several centuries passed since the word "Hades" first appeared in the Septuagint translation. Then in the third century CE, Neoplatonism, a strand of Platonic philosophy, started to rise in popularity.

> Plato made several philosophical arguments that have ironically come to define our mainstream Christian paradigms.

> 1. First, Plato believed that the soul was separate from the body and that the soul was fundamentally pure but tends to become deformed through association with the body.

6. McMillen, "A Biblical Staple."
7. McMillen, "A Biblical Staple."
8. McMillen, "A Biblical Staple."
9. McMillen, "A Biblical Staple."

2. Second, like his teacher Socrates, Plato believed that the soul itself was immortal, thus necessitating an eternal destination for the soul after the body dies.

3. Third, Plato proposed that good actions result in a reward in this life, but more importantly, a greater reward after death. Similarly, bad actions result in consequences in this life, but even greater punishment after death.

Plato linked some of his ideas to prevailing Greek mythology, including the locations of Hades and Tartarus. In Greek mythology, Tartarus is the location deep below Hades where the Titans were enslaved and the wicked were tormented. According to Plato, this is where divine punishment was meted out.[10]

Hades took on a new meaning. Once merely the residence of the dead, Hades became the place of eternal punishment. Hades became Hell. A piece of pagan mythology and philosophy became a doctrine of the church.

These ideas of the afterlife, which Christian leaders eventually found so tantalizing, were mocked by many pagan philosophers and writers. Seneca the Younger (4 BCE–65 CE) was a Stoic philosopher. About Hell, he writes, "Those things which make the infernal regions terrible, the darkness, the prison, the river of flaming fire, the judgment seat, etc., are all a fable, with which the poets amuse themselves, and by them agitate us with vain terrors."[11] The physician and philosopher Sextus Empiricus (160–210 CE) called them "poetic fables of hell," while Cicero, a Roman statesman (106–43 BCE) spoke of them as "silly absurdities and fables."[12]

AUGUSTINE AND NEO-PLATONISM

The concept of Hell as a place of eternal punishment slowly gained appeal and acceptance (especially in the Western or Latin side of the church) during the third and fourth centuries CE. It wasn't until Augustine, Bishop of Hippo, (354–430 CE) and his writings, though, that hell became accepted as church doctrine.[13] Augustine was one of the church's greatest theologians. His philosophical theology on original sin, free will, and the nature of humankind was heavily influenced by Neo-Platonism, however.[14] In his view

10. McMillen, "How and When."

11. Yeshua Before, "The Church's Development."

12. McMillian, "How and When."

13. McMillian, "How and When."

14. Livermore, "Augustine's Philosophical Theology."

of the afterlife, Augustine fully accepted the Neo-Platonic idea of the soul's eternal punishment. "Augustine not only said that hell was eternal for the wicked, but also for anyone who wasn't a Christian. So complete was his concept of God's exclusion of non-Christians that he considered unbaptized babies as damned. When these babies died, Augustine softened slightly to declare that they would be sent to the "upper level" of hell. Augustine is also the inventor of the concept of "hell lite," also known as *Purgatory*, which he developed to accommodate some of the universalist verses in the Bible."[15]

If asked, most Christians would profess that the doctrine of Hell as a place for the eternal punishment of the wicked is securely founded on Scripture. It is easy to see, however, that this is not true. The doctrine comes from pagan mythological and philosophical sources. When the Biblical writers were first inspired to pen the words "Sheol" and "Gehenna," these words had nothing to do with eternal damnation.

DANTE AND MILTON—IMAGES IN *DIVINE COMEDY* AND *PARADISE LOST*

Most Christians can describe hell in vivid terms. Hell is hot and is a place of many fires. It is almost volcanic in nature. Hell is a place of torture, torment, and pain—blood, sweat, and tears. There is no end to it. Water is not available to quench the constant thirst. Punishment is constant and remorseless. To make it worse, Satan and demons are the residents of Hell and the overseers of punishment for the wicked. They use pitchforks, whips, and chains to make a gruesome experience even more unbearable. Hell is a fearful place—one that is to be avoided at all costs.

It surprises people to realize that these images of Hell are not Biblically inspired. Besides the descriptions of Hades that come from pagan mythology, there are two main sources for the popular images of Hell and eternal damnation. The first is Dante Alighieri's (1265–1321 CE) *The Divine Comedy*. Dante's work is considered to be the pre-eminent work of Italian literature and one of the greatest works of world literature.[16] "In *The Divine Comedy*, Dante takes the reader through three realms of the dead: Hell, Purgatory, and Paradise. The poet has developed places for every type of person, allowing him to editorialize about people's actions in the world of his day. In the process, he creates vivid scenes of Hell, Purgatory, and Paradise. Those, then, became the basis for virtually all of the artistic depictions of hell in the

---

15. Vincent, "The Salvation Conspiracy."
16. Wikipedia, "Divine Comedy."

middle ages and our modern conceptions of a hell with demons, torment, and fire. All of it is poetry; none came from the Bible.[17]

The second work is John Milton's *Paradise Lost*. John Milton was a 17th century English writer, (1608–1674 CE). *Paradise Lost* is considered by critics to be Milton's greatest work and it helped establish Milton as one of the greatest English poets of his time.[18] "The poem concerns the Biblical story of the Fall of Man; the temptation of Adam and Eve by the fallen angel Satan and their expulsion from the Garden of Eden. Milton's purpose, stated in Book I, is to 'justify the ways of God to men.' "[19] His poem is filled with images, which have become common depictions of Hell. Again, great literature was used to bolster our concept of hell and eternal damnation. "If the church created hell, Dante and Milton furnished, decorated, and populated it. The church was delighted with the horrific images that would frighten the flock into submission and encourage conversion through fear, so it adopted them *in toto*. The fact that the images weren't biblical was a meaningless detail."[20]

A CONVENIENT TOOL—CONTROL WITHIN AND BEYOND THE CHURCH

We must ask ourselves why the doctrine of hell and eternal damnation appealed to the early church fathers and leaders of the church. What enticed them to so blatantly replace Jesus's message (God's kingdom of love and grace) with the threat of Hell, God's wrath, and unending punishment? The answer is surprisingly simple and so very human. It is control!

The church was not the first to come up with the idea that hell and the fear of punishment could be used to control people. This was one of the uses of Hades in its mythological and philosophical beginnings. Polybius, a Greek historian (200–118 BCE), commented on using these myths to control the people. He writes, "Since the multitude is ever fickle, full of lawless desires, irrational passions and violence, there is no other way to keep them in order but by the fear and terror of the invisible world; on which account our ancestors seem to me to have acted judiciously, when they contrived to bring into the popular belief these notions of the gods, and of the infernal regions."[21]

17. Wikipedia, "Divine Comedy."
18. Wikipedia, "Paradise Lost."
19. Wikipedia, "Paradise Lost."
20. Yeshua Before, "The Church's Development."
21. Yeshua Before, "The Church's Development."

Though separated by millennia, retired bishop John Shelby Spong would agree with this ancient historian. In a 2016 nationally televised interview, Spong shared his opinions on the church's use of this doctrine:

> I don't think Hell exists. I happen to believe in life after death, but I don't think it's got a thing to do with reward and punishment. Religion is always in the control business, and that's something people don't really understand. It's in a guilt-producing control business. And if you have Heaven as a place where you're rewarded for your goodness, and Hell is a place where you're punished for your evil, then you sort of have control of the population. And so they create this fiery place which has quite literally scared the Hell out of a lot of people, throughout Christian history. And it's part of a control tactic.[22]20

Anyone who has been a part of the church can bear witness to control exerted on people through the threat of hell and punishment. The threat of hell combined with the promise of a shorter experience in purgatory has raised countless millions of dollars for the church. Social norms and cultural mores have been established and enforced. What words, actions, and attitudes are moral and immoral have been defined. The normal and the different have been separated from those who are different and living under the threat of punishment. Even voting preferences have been determined by threatening judgment.

Bishop Spong believes Christians need to become critical in their thinking and mature in their faith so they can throw off the shackles of hell and damnation that have confined and controlled them. He states, **"The church doesn't like for people to grow up, because you can't control grown-ups . . .** [People] need to grow up. They need to accept their responsibility for themselves and the world."[23]

INSPIRATION OR IMAGINATION?— THE SPIRIT'S ABSENCE

The Bible is the inspired word of God. It is an authority for life and faith. The Bible, though, is not the source for the concepts of hell and eternal damnation. The church's doctrines on these topics have been built from the driftwood and debris of pagan mythology and philosophy. Eminent theologians and the greatest minds of the church developed these doctrines, for various

22. Spong, "Church Invented Hell."
23. Spong, "Church Invented Hell."

reasons. Still, in the final evaluation, the doctrines hell and eternal damnation are merely a figment of the church's imagination. They are not biblical, nor are they truth.

The cost of believing in these doctrines has been steep. The lies have distanced us from the truth. Jesus said that he has come to make us free, but we have been imprisoned by the fear of punishment. Rather than enjoying life in God's kingdom today, we have concerned ourselves with making it to heaven after we die. The gospel of Jesus Christ is a message from God that says, "I love you!" All too often we have heard the message of the church, "You're not good enough."

Jesus has a message for those of us who find ourselves battered and bruised—no matter what the cause. It is found in Matthew 11:28–30. Jesus says, "Come to me, all you that are weary and are carrying heavy burdens, and I will give you rest. Take my yoke upon you, and learn from me; for I am gentle and humble in heart, and you will find rest for your souls. For my yoke is easy, and my burden is light." We can find rest from the fear of Hell. As we will learn in the following chapters, we will also find rest from the fear of judgment.

4

Judgment in the Bible

Not Retribution and Not Everlasting

THE GARDEN OF EDEN—NO THREAT OF HELL

Though not an original biblical concept, we have uncovered how hell was transplanted into the Bible from pagan sources. We have also seen how hell and eternal damnation became dominant church doctrines. The main purpose of these doctrines was to incite fear and enable the church to control its members. The proclamation the good news of God's love and grace and the spread of God's kingdom has been curtailed. Instead, the church has used its resources to lift up the threat of punishment to strengthen and enrich itself.

In addition to the references to Hell (Sheol, Gehenna, and Tartarus) in the Bible, there are also several passages of judgment. Rebellion against God, the worship of other gods, and cruelty toward others result in God's judgment. What are we to do with these passages?

First, let us begin where Hell isn't. We don't find it in the Garden of Eden. The story is well-known; it is found in the second and third chapters of Genesis. After God creates the earth and the heavens, God scoops up dirt, breathes life into it and calls God's craft project Adam. God takes a rib from Adam's side and creates Eve, Adam's companion. God then places the couple in a garden called Eden.

The garden is filled with fruit trees ripe for the picking. Adam and Eve are free to have their fill of the trees' fruit. There is one tree, however, on which the Lord puts a "Do Not Pick the Fruit" sign. It is the tree of the knowledge of good and evil. Unfortunately, the fruit of the tree was very tempting. The fruit was good for food and a delight to the eyes. The woman, Eve, yields to the temptation of the serpent. She eats the forbidden fruit from the tree and Adam willingly follows suit.

We can all identify with Adam and Eve. We have burned our fingers after our parents told us not to touch the hot burner on the stove. A few of us have paint on our hands from the time when we saw the park bench with the "Don't touch, wet paint," sign on it.

Biblical scholars and theologians have offered many interpretations of the story of Adam and Eve. Some point out our human propensity to rebel and assert our independence. Others highlight our desire to be like God and be lord of our lives. Scholars in the Calvinistic or Reformed branch of the Christian Church use this story to develop their doctrine of total depravity. This is to say that there is no good in us and it is impossible for humans to please God. Most Biblical scholars and theologians do not interpret this story from that perspective, and it is a doctrine that is foreign to Jewish scholars.

After their act of rebellion, Adam and Eve hear God walking in the garden. The couple realizes that they are naked, and they hide. God finds the couple, confronts them with their sin, and punishes them. The woman will have pain in childbirth and the man will need to work hard to provide for his family and himself (Gen 3:16–19). The Lord banishes Adam and Eve from the Garden of Eden and places cherubim with flaming swords outside the garden's gates to prevent access to the tree of life.

A major change has taken place in the relationship between God and humankind. Adam and Eve are not living the life they were created to live. The relationship between God and God's creation has been bruised and some would say broken.

Notice, though, what isn't a part of the story. There is no hell; no threat of eternal punishment. In the view of some people, if any a couple ever deserved to be punished with eternal damnation, Adam and Eve would be that couple. They did, after all, according to the story, allow sin to enter the world. With sin came its fruits; suffering and death.

THE TEN COMMANDMENTS—NO ETERNAL PUNISHMENT

The book of Genesis ends with the Israelites surviving drought and famine by migrating to Egypt. There the author of Genesis records, "Thus Israel settled in the land of Egypt, in the region of Goshen; and they gained possessions in it, and were fruitful and multiplied exceedingly living and prospering in Egypt" (Gen 47:27). Though the Israelites prospered in Egypt, there was always the expectation that they would return to the land promised to their ancestor Abraham. They had no idea, however, how long it would be before they accomplished that feat. Nor did they imagine how dire their circumstances would become.

Several generations passed between the end of Genesis and the first chapters of Exodus. There is a new Pharaoh and the Israelites have prospered to such a degree that they are perceived as a threat by the Egyptians. To deal with the menace, the Pharaoh places the Israelites in harsh servitude and orders a draconian birth control program. God's people cry out for the Lord to save them and, after years of hearing their cries, the Lord moves to answer their prayers.

The Lord calls Moses, a shepherd with a history that is both privileged and violent, to lead God's people out of Egypt and into the Promised Land. After ten plagues, the Pharaoh decides that it is in his best interest to release the enslaved population, and he does so. The Israelites escape from Egypt and begin their journey through the Sinai desert to the land promised to Abraham, Isaac, and Jacob.

About three months after the Israelites had escaped from their enslavement in Egypt, they arrived at Mount Sinai. The Lord spoke to Moses and said to him, "You have seen what I did to the Egyptians, and how I bore you on eagles' wings and brought you to myself. Now therefore, if you obey my voice and keep my covenant, you shall be my treasured possession out of all the peoples. Indeed, the whole earth is mine, but you shall be for me a priestly kingdom and a holy nation" (Exod 19:4–6). Moses conveyed God's words to the elders of the people. They readily agreed to keep the covenant with God.

The Lord descended upon the mountain in a dense cloud. God then summoned Moses to climb up the mountain and enter into God's presence. While standing before God, Moses received the Ten Commandments. After the commandments were inscribed in stone, Moses then brought the commandments down to the people. Something is missing in this story, though. Nowhere in the narrative is there the threat of being cast into Hell and eternally punished—even when the Israelites rebel against God's covenant with them.

The writer of the book of Exodus records this rebellion in Exodus 32. Moses is delayed on Mount Sinai. The people grew anxious and impatient. In their fear, they persuaded Aaron to make a golden calf for them to worship. The next day they offered sacrifices to the idol and worshiped the golden calf. They reverted to the religions of Egypt.

The Lord was more than angry. God wanted to destroy the people (to send them to Sheol, not to hell). Moses interceded and pointed out that the Lord had made a covenant with Abraham, Isaac, and Israel. The Lord relented. The people were punished, though. Moses ground up the golden calf, mixed it with water, and forced the people to drink the potion. Later the sons of Levi executed around three thousand people. The punishment was harsh, but it never included condemnation and eternal torture in Hell.

Still, even though there is no word "Hell" in the Bible, there does seem to be many references to judgment and condemnation. How are we to understand and interpret these passages? Their presence may cause some to continue to doubt the claim that hell is a figment of the church's theological imagination.

A LIVING HELL—PRESENT NOT FUTURE TENSE

One instance in which Jesus mentions Gehenna is Matthew 5:30, "And if your right hand causes you to sin, cut it off and throw it away; it is better for you to lose one of your members than for your whole body to go into hell." There may be a few literalists who understand Jesus intended his instruction to be followed word for word. Most, however, (thankfully) interpret Jesus as speaking metaphorically. Jesus is not instructing his followers to cut off offending limbs or to gouge out eyes that have seen what they shouldn't have seen, or else face eternal punishment. Rather, Jesus is speaking about the power of sin in our lives—sin can bring hell into our lives and make our lives hellish.

The author of the letter of James shares this same thought when he writes, "And the tongue is a fire. The tongue is placed among our members as a world of iniquity; it stains the whole body, sets on fire the cycle of nature, and is itself set on fire by hell (Gehenna)" (Jas 3:6).

Jesus's and James's words are not theoretical in nature. We all know the power of sin in our lives. We have all experienced how the lack of forgiveness has bruised or destroyed our relationships with others. The effects of adultery on marriage relationships and families is common knowledge. The hell of addiction in all its various forms has touched our lives in one way or another. The pain and suffering, death and destruction that we can call hell are real. Hell is part of this life. It is not a part of life after death and it is not a place of eternal condemnation and suffering.

A GNASHING OF TEETH—A RESPONSE
OF THE RELIGIOUS

The mistranslation of words that were never intended to communicate a place of judgment and eternal punishment, along with the appropriation of pagan philosophy and mythology, are two elements that have led us to our common misunderstanding of hell. In addition to this, there are phrases such as "the weeping, gnashing of teeth and outer darkness," which at first glance appear to convey the idea of eternal punishment. Jesus speaks these words in Matthew 8, 13, 22, 24, 25 and Luke.[1]

The story of the Centurion and his sick servant is recorded in Matthew 8. When Jesus was in Capernaum, a Roman Centurion approached him with the request to heal his servant who was paralyzed and in terrible distress (Matt 8:6). Jesus replied that he would go immediately to the Centurion's home. The Centurion's response to Jesus's offer surprised Jesus. As a military man, the Centurion was well aware of the "chain of command." He was a man of authority who saw that Jesus was a man of ultimate authority. From this perspective, the Centurion told Jesus that Jesus didn't need to come to his house. All Jesus needed to do was to say the word and it would be done—the Centurion's servant would be healed.

Jesus was astonished by the depth of faith demonstrated by the Centurion, especially when he compared it to the lack of faith that he had experienced as he had proclaimed the arrival of God's kingdom and sought to minister to the needs of the people. Jesus said, "Truly I tell you, in no one in Israel have I found such faith. I tell you, many will come from east and west and will eat with Abraham and Isaac and Jacob in the kingdom of heaven, while the heirs of the kingdom will be thrown into the outer darkness, where there will be weeping and gnashing of teeth" (Matt 8:10–11).

It is interesting to note the identity of those who Jesus proclaims will be thrown into the outer darkness—the heirs of the kingdom. These are the religious people—the scribes, Pharisees, Sadducees, and priests—to whom Jesus is referring. When viewed in this light, it can be seen that Jesus is affirming that the kingdom of God will include non-Jews—Gentiles—those coming from the east and the west. The Jewish purists will be upset about this, bemoan their situation and gnash their teeth. Yes, there will be suffering, but it will not include eternal punishment and torment in Hell.

This uncomfortableness and dissatisfaction demonstrated by gnashing teeth can be seen in other passages. Stephen was one of the leaders of the early church. He was also the church's first martyr. He was brought before the

---

1. McMillen, "A Biblical Staple."

Sanhedrin and, in his defense, he enraged the religious authorities. Stephen accused them, saying, "You stiff-necked people, uncircumcised in heart and ears, you are forever opposing the Holy Spirit, just as your ancestors used to do. Which of the prophets did your ancestors not persecute? They killed those who foretold the coming of the Righteous One, and now you have become his betrayers and murderers. You are the ones that received the law as ordained by angels, and yet you have not kept it" (Acts 7:51–53).

Luke, the author of the Book of Acts, records the response of the members of the Sanhedrin. Luke states, "When they heard these things, they became enraged and ground their teeth at Stephen" (Acts 7:54). The grinding or gnashing of their teeth was a present-moment sign of anguish; they did not like what they had heard.

Jesus was accused of associating with tax collectors and sinners. He did. The accusations of the ruling class were justified. Jesus, however, never told the tax collectors, sinners, or the sick and possessed people that they would experience weeping, gnashing teeth, or the outer darkness.

Luke records Jesus's visit to Jericho. When Jesus entered the city, he saw Zacchaeus, a tax collector, perched in a tree. Jesus pointed to Zacchaeus and told him that he was going to come to Zacchaeus's home and visit him. Zacchaeus was so touched by Jesus's love and acceptance that he declared he would give away his riches. Jesus's words to Zacchaeus were, "Today salvation has come to this house, because he too is a son of Abraham. 10 For the Son of Man came to seek out and to save the lost" (Luke 19:1–10).

In another story, found in the gospel of John, Jesus is teaching in the temple. He is interrupted by a group of scribes and Pharisees that placed before him a woman caught in the act of adultery. Such a sin was punishable by stoning to death. The scribes and Pharisees wanted to see what Jesus would do. They were hoping that they could trap Jesus, prove him to be a sham, and bring some charges against him. Jesus draws in the dirt and says to all those who were standing around him that whoever was without sin could cast the first stone. Convicted, they all wander away until only Jesus and the woman were left. With her accusers gone, Jesus said to her, "Neither do I condemn you. Go your way, and from now on do not sin again" (John 8:1–10).

Jesus spoke words of comfort to the outcasts and those whom the "religious" people considered unworthy of God's love and grace. Jesus's statements about gnashing teeth were always spoken to the religious elite. They were words of warning to religious hypocrites.

THE JUDGMENT OF THE RIGHTEOUS—
OUTSIDERS ARE NOT CONDEMNED

Jesus continues his criticism (and his use of judgmental language) of the religious in name but not in deed, in a parable that has been entitled, "The Judgment of the Nations." This parable is found in Matthew 25:31–46. Some people believe that this is a prophetic statement from Jesus. This is to say that Jesus was describing a future event: there will be a time when people will stand before the throne of God and be judged for their works. A majority of biblical scholars and interpreters understand this passage to be a parable. A parable is not based on fact. It does not predict the future. Rather, a parable is a story that is meant to communicate a theological principle.

The setting of the parable comes after the Son of Man (Jesus) has returned in all of his glory. He sits upon his throne and all the nations are gathered before him. The people are separated into two groups: the sheep and the goats, with the sheep on his right and the goats on his left. The Son of Man turns to the people on his right and proclaims that they will inherit the kingdom—heaven. These people—the sheep—are later called "the righteous" (verse 37). They are righteous because, "I [The Son of Man] was hungry and you gave me food, I was thirsty and you gave me something to drink, I was a stranger and you welcomed me, I was naked and you gave me clothing, I was sick and you took care of me, I was in prison and you visited me" (Matt 25:35–36). The sheep are caught off guard. They don't remember ever giving the Son of Man food, drink, and clothing, or caring for him when he was sick. The Son of Man clarifies their confusion by saying, "Truly I tell you, just as you did it to one of the least of these who are members of my family, you did it to me" (Matt 25:40).

The Son of Man then turns to those on his left—the goats—and calls them "accursed." In this parable, The Son of Man condemns them to the eternal fire prepared for the devil and his angels (verse 41) and to eternal punishment (verse 46). The reason that they are condemned to such a fate is that, "I [the Son of Man] was hungry and you gave me no food, I was thirsty and you gave me nothing to drink, I was a stranger and you did not welcome me, naked and you did not give me clothing, sick and in prison and you did not visit me" (Matt 25:42–43).

This certainly was a scene that would resonate with the people to whom Jesus was speaking. To those people who considered themselves to be religious, Jesus's words were disconcerting, and perhaps they felt his words even contained a strong note of condemnation. As has been pointed out earlier, the appropriation of Hades and eternal judgment of a person's good or bad works, by this time, had been appropriated by the dominant culture.

This, however, is not the good news proclaimed by Jesus and by the writers of the New Testament.

Christians understand that everyone has sinned and fallen short of the glory of God. In a key passage in his Letter to the Romans, Paul writes, "But God proves his love for us in that while we still were sinners Christ died for us. Much more surely then, now that we have been justified by his blood, will we be saved through him from the wrath of God. For if while we were enemies, we were reconciled to God through the death of his Son, much more surely, having been reconciled, will we be saved by his life" (Rom 5:8–10). We celebrate along with Paul the truth: while we were yet sinners Jesus died for us and through his death and resurrection we have been reconciled to God. Our works do not justify us before God; we do not work hard to get to heaven. Instead, we live by faith. Paul writes to the Ephesians and proclaims to them, "For by grace you have been saved through faith, and this is not your own doing; it is the gift of God—not the result of works, so that no one may boast. For we are what he has made us, created in Christ Jesus for good works, which God prepared beforehand to be our way of life (Eph 2:8–10).

Far from being a prediction of a cosmic event, this "Parable of the Nations" is a strong warning to those who consider themselves to be religious and righteous people, but who do not live out their religion in love and care for others. "Watch out," Jesus is saying. "A life of faith is more than attending worship services, Bible studies, and pot-luck dinners." In those verses to the Ephesians, Paul declares that we have been created for good works. We have been created to care for each other. James says it well in his letter when he writes, "Show me your faith apart from your works, and I by my works will show you my faith" (Jas 2:18).

CORRECTIVE PUNISHMENT FOR AN AGE—NOTHING EVERLASTING

There still may be some people who are uncomfortable with those words about eternal fire and eternal punishment. Again, like the word "hell" the traditional concept of eternal punishment is based on poor translations. "The word "punishment" used here is "iskolasis," which can also be translated as "correction." It speaks to the idea of corrective punishment.[2] "The word "eternal" used here is the Greek word, "aiōnios," and like Gehenna, it has been completely mistranslated throughout the New Testament.[3] New Testament Greek teacher Richard Liantonio explains, "In Greek, an Age

2. McMillen, "A Biblical Staple."

3. Liantonio, "Why Greek Matters."

could refer to a generation, lifetime, or a longer, finite length of time. It's where we get our word "eon." It also correlates with the Hebrew word "Yom," which denotes anything from a 24-hour period to an epoch season."[4]

The idea of correction for a specific time is quite different from one of eternal punishment and torment. One is reflective of loving parents, who seek to guide their children to become loving and caring individuals. Bad behavior is punished so that it might be replaced by good behavior. A pre-school student who hits another in a fit of anger may be placed in a corner for a "time out." A teen-ager may be grounded for breaking curfew. Young people are not banished from the family, thrown out of the house, and relegated to the streets forever for bringing home a "C" on a report card. Such an action is not reflective of good parenting, nor is it similar eternal punishment an action that is consistent with the character of God. God is a loving God. Even a just God can be understood to work with restorative punishment instead of retributive punishment.

This type of restorative punishment is seen in the Hebrew Scriptures in the Lord's interaction with God's wayward people. During the period of the Judges, the Israelites had an on-again, off-again relationship with God. The historians who recorded the events in the book of Judges believed God would allow the Israelites to be subjugated by the nations that surrounded them as punishment for their infidelity to God. Eventually, the Israelites would realize the error of their ways and turn to God, repent of their unfaithfulness, and ask God to deliver them. Since God's intention was always restorative punishment rather than retributive punishment, God would send a charismatic leader called a judge to deliver them from their predicament.

Throughout Israel's history, the prophets would call the people to turn from their worship of false gods and idols and renew their relationship with the one, true God. Their failure to do so eventually resulted in their defeat by the Babylonian army and their exile to Babylon. The People of God lost everything. They no longer had their homes, possessions, and lands. They even lost the Temple, which was understood as God's presence in their lives. This punishment, which some call the Babylonian Captivity, lasted for several decades. Eventually, though, the people of God returned to the Promised Land and rebuilt their lives—and the Temple. Again, it can be seen that God's punishment of the nation was restorative in nature.

Even the story of Noah and the Flood appears restorative. God did grieve over the wickedness of humankind (Gen 6:6). God decided to blot out humankind with a flood. Noah, however, found favor in God's sight. The

---

4. Liantonio, "Why Greek Matters."

flood, though harsh, became a reboot for humankind that enabled people to turn from their wickedness and walk in a relationship with God.

The parable of Lazarus and the Rich Man found in Luke 16:19–31, provide us with the only visual of afterlife torment found in Scripture. For many Christians, this passage is the undeniable truth that there is a hell with condemnation and eternal torment. To interpret this passage in this manner evades the fact that this is a parable of Jesus. This passage of Scripture is a story. It is not meant to be an exposé of life after death. Its original intent was to serve as a criticism of society's neglect of the poor and needy (especially by the rich and the religious).

There are several arguments to support the difficulty of using this parable to describe what the afterlife will be like. One of them is the timing of the scene. Orthodox Christians believe that there will be a resurrection of the dead at the time of Jesus' return. After the resurrection, there will be a time of judgment when the righteous will enter heaven and the unrighteous will be condemned to hell. In this parable, the resurrection has not taken place.

> Moreover, aspects of the story make a crass literalism awkward: how does the rich man communicate with Abraham across the chasm? Does everyone there have a direct line to the patriarch? Does someone being incinerated in a furnace care about thirst? Are these literal flames? And since *hades* precedes the resurrection of the body, do we have literal tongues with which to feel thirst? Is this also the literal Abraham? Do the millions in his care take turns snuggling with him? Or is his bosom big enough to contain us all at once? How big he must be! And so on into implausibility.[5]

The last scenes of supposed eternal punishment that we will look at are "the Lake of Fire" passages in Revelation. There is a total of five such passages. They are found in Revelation chapters 19, 20, and 21.[6]

The book of Revelation falls into a category called Apocalyptic. Apocalyptic literature "is a type of genre that is very much symbolic and cryptic. Symbols are usually culturally developed and must be interpreted using that culture's perspective or lens."[7] This means that we cannot interpret the book of Revelation literally. If we do, we are guaranteed to interpret it incorrectly.

What we can do is understand that the book of Revelation is a symbolic description of the classic battle of good versus evil. The book describes this conflict using figures from creation mythology such as sea monsters,

5. McMillen, "A Biblical Staple."
6. McMillen, "A Biblical Staple."
7. McMillen, "A Biblical Staple."

waters of chaos, and supernatural creatures. In the end, good is victorious over evil and evil is destroyed. In the book of Daniel, which is another apocalyptic book, we read, "I watched then because of the noise of the arrogant words that the horn was speaking. And as I watched, the beast was put to death, and its body destroyed and given over to be burned with fire" (Dan 7:11). Similarly, Revelation records, "And the devil who had deceived them was thrown into the lake of fire and sulfur, where the beast and the false prophet were, and they will be tormented day and night forever and ever" (Rev 20:10).

The epic battle portrayed in the book of Revelation describes God's victory over sin, death, and evil. This is good news! It was especially good news to the Christians of the early church who faced persecution and death. Those early Christians witnessed the power of Rome and their own human weakness. In their eyes, the situation might have appeared hopeless; Evil would defeat Good. The message of the book of Revelation brought a word of hope to those early Christians. The book of Revelation continues to whisper the good news (that God will defeat evil) to all those who see themselves in hopeless situations or who fear the evil in the world will overcome the good. In the face of insurmountable opposition, we can shout along with the early Christians who first heard the proclamation of the book of Revelations, "Amen. Come, Lord Jesus! (Rev 21:20). Hell does not threaten us, but the love of God empowers us.

5

God's Justice

Moving Toward Restoration

ATTRACTIVENESS OF REVENGE—
OUR QUEST FOR JUSTICE

I hope by now you have been convinced beyond a reasonable doubt there is no hell; it is a figment of the church's theological imagination. If not, I hope that the arguments against hell and eternal punishment have at least caused you to begin to think about the possibility. The absence of hell and eternal punishment, though, brings up another difficult question for us to consider: "What happens to all of the bad people?"

There are some people we sincerely hope would go to hell. There are our neighbors who party and play loud music until the wee hours of the night. The gal who was busy texting, cut us off in traffic, and almost caused an accident deserves eternal punishment. When we were in high school, there was the class bully who made our lives a living hell. Surely, he and his minions warrant roasting forever—even if it is on medium heat. The list could go on and on. There are scores of people who not only do not know Jesus but whose actions deserve God's condemnation.

On a more serious note, there are people whose eternal destiny we do question. There are the priests in the Roman Catholic Church who for decades sexually preyed upon young boys and girls. For the most part, they have escaped punishment. Will they encounter God's condemnation and be tortured eternally for what they have done? Certainly, we believe they deserve it.

The #metoo movement has brought to light the truth that women have experienced and endured sexual abuse and molestation at the hands of men. Some men have been labeled "predators." A few of these men have been brought to trial, have been convicted of their crimes, and are now serving out jail sentences. People have celebrated that justice finally has prevailed. Others have escaped punishment. Will they eventually receive their come-uppance at the hands of God?

There's the driver who had two previous DUI convictions. On a sus-pended license, he decided to drive again with a blood alcohol reading twice the legal limit. He lost control of his car while driving on the high-way, crossed over the median, and hit a minivan containing a family of five. The drunk driver and all the members of the family were killed. What will happen to him? Several schools in the United States have been invaded by gun-wielding assassins. Scores of innocent young lives have been cut short. Will justice ever be served?

Some people are universally condemned, such as serial killers Ted Bundy, John Wayne Gacy, and Jeffrey Dahmer. World leaders like Joseph Stalin, Adolf Hitler, and Pol Pot killed millions of people. They have been judged harshly by historians and by the generations that followed them. Osama bin Laden, members of Al Qaida, the Taliban, ISIS, and other ter-rorist groups might also be added to the list. What is their eternal destiny? We know what we would like to happen. We want justice to prevail. We want the bad to be punished and the good to be rewarded. We want things to be made right.

Capital punishment is still practiced in several states in the United States. It usually takes several years, maybe decades, for a convicted criminal to work through the various legal processes and finally be executed. Though the death of their loved ones occurred many, many years ago, the victim's family members will say that the death of the criminal finally gave them closure. Justice has been done; "An eye for an eye, a tooth for a tooth . . . ." (Exod 21:24)—and a life for a life.

The concept of hell was not simply foisted on an unsuspecting public. Hell served a purpose for the masses. Hell promised justice—at least what we would term justice. Evil people may prosper and escape the long arm of the law, but eventually, at the end of time, they would be judged and justice would be served. Conversely, the righteous may suffer; they may be poor, persecuted, and neglected. They could persevere, though, knowing that they would be rewarded. St. Paul said it well, "I consider that the sufferings of this present time are not worth comparing with the glory about to be revealed to us" (Rom 8:18).

Many people rejoice over the idea that there is no hell. They are glad to learn that hell is the product of poor translations, the adaptation of pagan philosophy and mythology, and a concerted effort by the Church to control people. Many others have a gut reaction against the thought that there is no hell. They not only rebel against the idea that they have been fooled and have believed a lie—these people also know the church's teachings on hell helped them survive in an unjust world. Their focus has not been on the transient nature of this world, but rather on the future and the promise of what is to come.

A DIFFERENT DEFINITION OF JUSTICE— GOD'S WAY, NOT OUR WAY

The reaction that many people have in learning that there is no hell is similar to what they felt when O.J. Simpson was acquitted of murdering Nicole Brown and Ron Goldman. Outrage! As human beings, we crave a world that is just. To assure that justice is served, we have listed the characteristic of "just" as one of the key characteristics of God. God is loving, gracious, merciful, AND just.

The problem is that God's definition of justice is different than ours. While Jesus was carrying out his ministry on earth, he acted in many ways that were counter to the social mores of his time. Jesus considered the practices unjust; Jesus was criticized for his actions. One of the criticisms leveled against Jesus by the religious aristocracy was that he was a glutton and a drunkard, a friend of tax collectors and sinners (Luke 7:34). A Pharisee by the name of Simon invited Jesus to dinner. During the meal, a sinful woman came up to Jesus and poured expensive perfume over his feet and then washed his feet with her tears and dried them with her hair. We don't know in what way the woman was sinful, though we can guess. She had a reputation, which Simon knew. Simon thought, as a prophet, Jesus also should have known what the woman was. Simon assumed that with such knowledge Jesus wouldn't have allowed the woman to touch him. Instead of condemning her, though, Jesus commends the woman's great love for him. At the same time, Jesus turns the table and criticizes Simon for his failure to show Jesus rudimentary acts of hospitality (Luke 7:36–50).

If Jesus was a just messiah, he wouldn't have healed a Centurion's servant—a hated Roman oppressor—or reached out to several lepers, touched them, and healed them. A just, religious person would not have cast out an evil spirit from a man on the Sabbath, nor would he have healed a man with a withered hand.

The Jewish religious leaders and Roman government officials believed that it was perfectly just to send a potential rabble-rouser and threat to their power and wealth to the cross. On the other hand, God sought justice—to bring humankind into a justified relationship with God—through the life, death, and resurrection of Jesus. God never punishes simply to punish. God punishes to restore a relationship.

PUNISHMENT TO RESTORE RELATIONSHIPS— BIBLICAL AND EXPERIENTIAL

Throughout Jesus's ministry, he sought to restore relationships. Lepers were socially and religiously unclean. Jesus reached out, touched them, cleansed them, and restored them to their community, enabling them to again participate in temple worship. The lame, blind, and sick were considered not only unclean but also judged by God because of something they had done. Jesus healed them and removed the stigma of the sickness and any reason for viewing them as judged by God. Women, at the time of Jesus, were considered objects to be owned. Women who were menstruating (or hemorrhaging [Luke 8:43]) were considered unclean. Jesus treated women as equals. He had friends such as Mary and Martha and Mary Magdalene. As with men, Jesus reached out to women, healed them, made them clean, and restored them to their communities and families. Of course, the greatest example of Jesus restoring relationships is his work on the cross. As John writes in his gospel, "Indeed, God did not send the Son into the world to condemn the world, but in order that the world might be saved through him" (John 3:17).

Christians have always understood Jesus's actions to be demonstrative of God's characteristics. Priest and author Richard Rohr poses the question, "Why would Jesus's love be so unconditional while he was in this world, and suddenly become totally conditional after death"[1] It doesn't make sense. As followers of Jesus, we are called to love one another as Jesus has loved us (John 13:35). We are also instructed to forgive others. Jesus, in a conversation with Peter, responded to Peter's question of how many times he should forgive others. Jesus answered Peter by telling him to forgive seventy times seven or, in other words, don't stop forgiving (Matt 18:22). Again, Richard Rohr poses the question, "How could Jesus ask us to bless, forgive, and heal

---

1. Rohr, *Falling Upward*, 102.

our enemies, which he clearly does (Matthew 5:43–48), unless God is doing it first and always.[2]

From the moment of humankind's rebellion against God (Adam and Eve), God's goal has been to restore the relationship God had with God's creation. In his Sermon on the Mount, Jesus tells his disciples and the crowds, "Be perfect, therefore, as your heavenly Father is perfect" (Matt 5:48). This is a poor translation that has caused immense grief in the lives of millions of Christians who have tried unsuccessfully to be perfect. The Greek word is *telos*, which can be (better) translated as "complete," or "finished." When an artist is finished with the painting or sculpture, that work of art can be described as *telos*, or complete. It has reached its finished state. In his letter, James writes about the complete or finished state of the followers of Jesus. He states, "My brothers and sisters, whenever you face trials of any kind, consider it nothing but joy, because you know that the testing of your faith produces endurance; and let endurance have its full effect, so that you may be mature and complete, lacking in nothing" (Jas 1:2–4). James sees the Holy Spirit using the trials and struggles of the early Christians to draw them "closer" in their relationship with God. As the early Christians lived in the reality of God's relationship with them and rested more and more in God's embrace, they were *telos*—complete people. Their completeness was in God. Elizabeth Eaton, the presiding bishop of the Evangelical Lutheran Church in America, sums it up in this manner: "Jesus was clear that when he is raised up, he will draw all people to himself. Ever since we got booted out of the garden, it has been God's relentless pursuit to bring his people to God."[3]

NOT "IN HELL," RATHER "IN ME"— DANCING WITH THE TRINITY

For over fifteen hundred years, the church has gotten the message of the Bible wrong. It is not "in hell," but rather, "in me." One of the criminals who was crucified with Jesus asked Jesus to remember him when Jesus came into his kingdom. Jesus replied that the criminal would be with him that day in paradise. The emphasis of the statement was not the word "paradise" but rather "with me."[4] Paul writes to the Philippians that his desire is "to depart and be with Christ, for that is far better" (Philippians 1:23). ". . .Instead of speculating about life after death, Paul puts the emphasis on being 'with Christ.' Thus, Jesus's promise to the thief and Paul's yearning remind us of

2. Rohr, *Falling Upward*, 103.

3. Eaton, "By the Light," 14.

4. Wengert, "By the Light," 15.

the single most important thing about life after death *and* about the resurrection of the dead: We will be with Christ."[5]

There are perhaps hundreds of verses in the Bible proclaiming God's plan to save all. Here are a few:

> will bless those who bless you, and the one who curses you I will curse; and in you all the families of the earth shall be blessed" (Gen 12:3).

> "On this mountain the LORD of hosts will make for all peoples
> a feast of rich food, a feast of well-aged wines,
> of rich food filled with marrow, of well-aged wines strained clear.
> And he will destroy on this mountain
> the shroud that is cast over all peoples,
> the sheet that is spread over all nations." (Isa 25:6–8)

> "Do not be afraid; for see—I am bringing you good news of great joy for all the people:11 to you is born this day in the city of David a Savior, who is the Messiah, the Lord" (Luke 2:10–11).

> "I do not judge anyone who hears my words and does not keep them, for I came not to judge the world, but to save the world" (John 12:47).

> "In that renewal there is no longer Greek and Jew, circumcised and uncircumcised, barbarian, Scythian, slave and free; but Christ is all and in all" (Col 3:11) and,

> "Lord, who will not fear
> and glorify your name?
> For you alone are holy.
> All nations will come
> and worship before you,
> for your judgments have been revealed" (Rev 15:4).

In answer to our opening question "What happens to bad people?," we can answer with certainty that they will not be condemned and exiled to hell for an eternity of punishment. Rather, in some way, shape, and form they will be "with God." This is good news for all the people of the world who have been deemed bad people by the world's other occupants. It is also good news for the rest of us. For we, like them, have sinned and fallen short

5. Wengert, "By the Light," 15.

of the glory of God (Rom 3:23). We can bemoan our human state, like Paul when he writes:

> I do not understand my own actions. For I do not do what I want, but I do the very thing I hate. Now if I do what I do not want, I agree that the law is good. But in fact it is no longer I that do it, but sin that dwells within me. For I know that nothing good dwells within me, that is, in my flesh. I can will what is right, but I cannot do it. For I do not do the good I want, but the evil I do not want is what I do. Now if I do what I do not want, it is no longer I that do it, but sin that dwells within me.
>
> So I find it to be a law that when I want to do what is good, evil lies close at hand. For I delight in the law of God in my inmost self, but I see in my members another law at war with the law of my mind, making me captive to the law of sin that dwells in my members.24 Wretched man that I am! Who will rescue me from this body of death? (Rom 7:15–24)

We may get angry at the people who cut in front of us in traffic, but we have done this, too. Bullying may anger us, yet we have used our power over others in a wrongful manner. We have also stood by, in a cowardly fashion, while others have been bullied, marginalized, or neglected. It is easy for us to condemn evil people like Hitler and Stalin, while we live lives of conspicuous consumers and neglect the hungry and the homeless. Terrorists are vilified because they have killed innocent people. We have done this, too. As nations at war, we have killed innocent bystanders and have labeled them "collateral damage." We hate those who are different than ourselves. We do not forgive those who have hurt us. To only those who first love us do we return love.

The good news of Jesus Christ and the message of the Bible is not that the evil people are going to be judged, found lacking, and condemned. The good news is that God is moving in our lives and in all of creation to bring all people to be with God.

UNIVERSALISM IS NOT NEW—THE EASTERN CHURCH FATHERS

The concept of Christian Universalism is not a new teaching. Many understand it to be central to the teachings of Jesus Christ. For example, he said that when he was lifted up (on the cross) that he would draw all men to himself (John 12:32). Paul, the author of several of the books of the New Testament also appears to have supported the concept of universal salvation.

"Paul created an intellectually coherent view of the meaning and message of Christ that was heavily focused around the teaching that through successive ages of time, God is in the process of bringing all beings back to Himself — that through the transformative influence of His firstborn Son, the Christ, all people can be raised up into the station of mature sons and daughters of God (e.g., see 1 Cor 15:22–28, 2 Cor 3:18, Gal. 4:4–5, Eph 5:1).[6]

Christian Universalism was certainly the understanding of many of the church fathers.

"The early church from the time of the Apostles until the 4th century was primarily a Universalist church. Most of the church fathers during this period believed that all people will be saved."[7] There were six schools (centers of theological and philosophical discussion) in the early church—from around 170 to 430 CE. Only one of these schools taught the doctrine of eternal torment and hell. That was the school in Carthage under Augustine. Four of the other five taught that, through the death and resurrection of Christ, all people would be saved through restorative judgment and reconciliation.[8]

The greatest theological school of the patristic period was located in Alexandria, Egypt. St. Clement was one of the leaders of the Alexandrian school (150–220 CE). He was a strong advocate of universal salvation. He wrote in his *Stromata* and *Pedagogue*:

> For all things are ordered both universally and in particular by the Lord of the universe, with a view to the salvation of the universe. But needful corrections, by the goodness of the great, overseeing judge, through the attendant angels, through various prior judgments, through the final judgment, compel even those who have become more callous to repent. . . . So He saves all; but some He converts by penalties, others who follow Him of their own will, and in accordance with the worthiness of His honor, that every knee may be bent to Him of celestial, terrestrial and infernal things (Phil. 2:10), that is angels, men, and souls who before his [Christ's] advent migrated from this mortal life. . . . For there are partial corrections (*paideiai*) which are called chastisements (*kolasis*), which many of us who have been in transgression incur by falling away from the Lord's people. But as children are chastised by their teacher, or their father, so are we by Providence. . . for good to those who are chastised collectively and individually.[9]

---

6. Rohr, "Patristic Period."
7. Christian Universalist, "History of Universalism."
8. Hanson, *Prevailing Doctrine*, 125.
9. Rohr, "Patristic Period."

A student of St. Clement and another leader of the Alexandrian School was Origen (185–254 CE). He was a proponent of Universal Salvation. He emphasized the teaching that all souls have emanated from God, descended into realms of separation as they fell into sin, and must ascend back to the Source of All Being through a divine plan of multiple ages and trials.[10]

In his *De Principiis* and *Against Celsus* concerning the way God will restore all beings to Himself, Origin wrote:

> God's consuming fire works with the good as with the evil, annihilating that which harms His children. This fire is one that each one kindles; the fuel and food is each one's sins. . . . When the soul has gathered together a multitude of evil works, and an abundance of sins against itself, at a suitable time all that assembly of evils boils up to punishment, and is set on fire to chastisement. . . [I]t is to be understood that God our Physician, desiring to remove the defects of our souls, should apply the punishment of fire. . . . Our God is a 'consuming fire' in the sense in which we have taken the word; and thus He enters in as a 'refiner's fire' to refine the rational nature, which has been filled with the lead of wickedness, and to free it from the other impure materials which adulterate the natural gold or silver, so to speak, of the soul. [O]ur belief is that the Word [Christ] shall prevail over the entire rational creation, and change every soul into his own perfection. . . . For stronger than all the evils in the soul is the Word, and the healing power that dwells in him; and this healing he applies, according to the will of God, to every man.[11]

Gregory of Nyssa was another church father who supported the idea of eternal salvation. Gregory lived from 335 to 395 CE. He was influential in the development of the doctrine of the Trinity and the Nicene Creed. He wrote, "For it is evident that God will in truth be all in all when there shall be no evil in existence, when every created being is at harmony with itself and every tongue shall confess that Jesus Christ is Lord; when every creature shall have been made one body."[12]

Bishop Theodore of Mopsuestia (350–428 CE) is a theologian and church leader from another area of the Christian church. He represents a branch that was centered in Antioch and Constantinople. Later this group of Christians would be identified as Nestorians. Bishop Theodore was an adamant supporter of Universal salvation. He emphasized the sovereignty

---

10. Rohr, "Patristic Period."
11. Rohr, "Patristic Period."
12. Rohr, "Patristic Period."

and power of God to restore all beings to Himself regardless of their free will to rebel. He wrote:

> The wicked who have committed evil the whole period of their lives shall be punished till they learn that, by continuing in sin, they only continue in misery. And when, by this means, they shall have been brought to fear God, and to regard Him with good will, they shall obtain the enjoyment of His grace. For He never would have said, 'until thou hast paid the uttermost far-thing,' [Mat. 5:26] unless we can be released from suffering after having suffered adequately for sin; nor would He have said, 'he shall be beaten with many stripes,' [Luke 12:47] and again, 'he shall be beaten with few stripes,' [vs. 48] unless the punishment to be endured for sin will have an end.[13]

Though the early church fathers express their belief in universal salvation, they also write about corrective punishments that will occur in this life and the next. These punishments will eventually bring the individual back into the relationship with God for which he or she was created. Theodore of Mopsuestia, as was previously quoted, wrote "The wicked . . . shall be punished till they learn that, by continuing in sin, they only continue in misery." Origen writes about a refiner's fire. St. Clement mentions "needed corrections." None of these punishments are everlasting. All of them have the purpose of fulfilling God's desire to bring everything under God's authority (1 Cor 15:28).

A key element to the concept of universal salvation and limited corrective punishment is the idea of eternity. Technically, eternity, everlasting, and eternal don't truly exist in the scripture.[14] In the Hebrew Scriptures, the word that has often been translated as "eternal" is the word "olam." Literally, the word means "behind the horizon" or "concealed from view." Though often translated "everlasting," a better translation is "age"—a period of time. This age is not infinite, but rather has a set beginning and end.[15]

Likewise in the New Testament, the word translated frequently as everlasting or eternal is the word "aion." From this word, we get the English word "eon."[16] An eon is a long time. It could be understood as an "age." It is a period that has a beginning and an end. So, a punishment that has been translated as "eternal" should really be understood as punishment for a time—an age.

13. Rohr, "Patristic Period."
14. Brazen Church, "How and When."
15. Ferwerda, *Raising Hell*, 145.
16. Ferwerda, *Raising Hell*, 145.

What about God? God is described as eternal. Doesn't translating "aion" as "age" place a limit on the timelessness of God? The short answer is, "No." "The use of the words by the original writers is merely describing one of God's many attributes as being the 'God of the ages,' reigning supreme over [God's] time-bound plan."[17]

What about the eternal life that we have been given through the life, death, and resurrection of Jesus? If in Matthew 25:46 we translate "eternal punishment" as an "age (eonian) of correction," what do we do with the "eternal life?" "Eonian life" is not eternal life. "It means coming into life (relationship with Jesus) in the age that the Bible writer is referring to and continuing through the remaining ages. In any age you live that you are connected to Jesus—the life source or "Vine"—you are enjoying life in that age."[18] The emphasis of eternal life is not on the length of time, or the age or ages. Rather, the focus is on the fact that we are with God. God has drawn all of creation to God.

CONSTANTINE—THE CHURCH
MOVES FROM EAST TO WEST

With its foundations in the teachings of Jesus, Paul, and the early church fathers, it is difficult to understand how universal salvation did not become the orthodox belief of the Christian Church. Seismic shifts, however, took place in the church, moving the Christian faith away from the teachings of Jesus and the church fathers of the East—transferring them to the west. These shifts took place in the fourth century CE.

The most significant event of the fourth century was the legalization of Christianity in 313 CE by the emperor Constantine. Previous to this, the Roman Empire had been viewed as an enemy to the Christian faith. Followers of the Way (Christians) had been a minority religious group that had been persecuted, tortured, and executed. Suddenly, enemies became friends and Christianity became the semi-official religion of the Roman Empire. What had once been discussions over theological differences escalated into political and theological infighting. Constantine intervened and, in an effort to establish a unified, orthodox belief structure, called an ecumenical council of bishops.[19]

The effect of these events moved the center of the church to Rome and the description of the Christian faith closer to the state—the Roman

17. Ferwerda, *Raising Hell*, 152.
18. Ferwerda, *Raising Hell*, 154.
19. Christian Universalist, "History of Universalism."

Empire. Church leaders became more interested in pleasing the political powers of Rome than they were in accurately interpreting the Scriptures and developing a theology true to the teachings of Jesus.[20] To create unity, dissidents were branded as heretics. The winners of the theological battles removed them from the Christian fellowship and placed them outside the "true" church.

Another shift was away from the influence of the Alexandrian school to the Carthage School. Augustine was the leader of the Carthage school and his writings became influential in the development of the teachings of the church and their distancing from the teachings of Jesus. "Augustine is considered the father of Western theology. He was responsible for a wholesale change in Christian thinking, replacing the belief system of the Apostles and most of the early church fathers with a completely different version of the gospel that has been handed down as the fundamental basis of much of Catholic and Protestant Christianity."[21] Augustine was a strong proponent of the Roman church's hierarchy and organization as the "visible kingdom of God on earth" and its role in law, politics, war, and government.[22]

At the insistence of the emperor Justinian, the bishops at the Second Council of Constantinople made Hell eternal by an official decree in 544 CE. The Christian theologian, Origen, was declared a heretic in 553 CE. Nestorian Christians were also named as heretics, as was anyone who disagreed with what was then identified as the orthodox Christian faith. "Many writings of Origen, his supporters, and Nestorian Universalists, such as Theodore of Mopsuestia were destroyed by church censors."[23]

We have a common assumption that orthodox beliefs, or right doctrine, miraculously appeared. We envision the Holy Spirit supernaturally revealing these doctrines such as Mary's virginity, Jesus's divinity, the Trinity, hell, and eternal punishment, and the leaders of the church unanimously accepted them. Nothing could be further from the truth. Certainly, the Holy Spirit could have joined the fray but, "The truth is that since the very beginning, church history has been rife with unrest, conflict, and even bloodshed—primarily over matters of establishing orthodoxy"[24] When one looks below the surface and studies the history of the church, the truth becomes apparent. The truth is "that for centuries, Christian Orthodoxy preserved

20. Christian Universalist, "History of Universalism."

21. Christian Universalist, "History of Universalism."

22. Christian Universalist, "History of Universalism."

23. Christian Universalist, "History of Universalism."

24. Brazen Church, "How and When."

itself through fear and control, opting to protect its doctrinal 'truth' through the active suppression of opposing ideas."[25]

The struggle for orthodoxy has been constant throughout the history of the church. The Protestant reformation attacked the orthodox practices of the selling of indulgences and works righteousness. The reformers recaptured Jesus's original teachings of God's love and grace, and Paul's understanding that humankind is saved by grace through faith (Eph 2:8).

Then the reformers argued about the proper understanding of communion and the correct application of baptism. Those items are still debated, though not as adamantly as in previous centuries.

Life in the church and the struggle over correct doctrine isn't much different today. As noted previously, since the 1960s the idea that only men can be leaders in the church has been challenged. Books, in support of both sides, have been written. Study materials have been published. Resolutions have been proposed, debated, and voted either up or down. Both sides believe they are interpreting the Scripture correctly. For the most part, the discussion and debate have been civil. Still, there have been intense arguments, harsh words, and bitter feelings. After over fifty years of discussion, about one-fourth of the Christian church ordains women and/or allows women into leadership positions.

The same thing is happening over gay rights. Arguments are intense over gay rights in the church and what is the right doctrine concerning the Queer Community. Congregations have been split over this controversy and so have denominations. A growing number of congregations believe that the Bible has very little to say about homosexuality. They also believe that to be true to Jesus's command to love one another as he has loved them, they need to be open and accepting of their LGBTQ neighbor. Other members of the Christian church cite some of the fourteen passages of scripture that refer to same-sex actions (cult prostitution and pederasty) to support the condemnation of same-sex relationships. Even though same-sex marriage has been declared to be constitutional in the United States, some denominations permit their clergy to officiate at such marriage ceremonies while other denominations do not.

Arguments against the orthodox belief of hell and eternal punishment are not new. Early in the history of the church, the idea of hell was mocked, and the teaching of eternal punishment was identified as pagan in origin. Early church fathers spoke and wrote in favor of universal salvation. Though condemned as heretics, with their writings destroyed or repressed, the counter-orthodox beliefs have continued in the life of the church. Recently

25. Brazen Church, "How and When."

the arguments against the doctrine of hell and eternal punishment have resurfaced, but books on the subject can be found dating back to the late nineteenth century.

Having established that hell and eternal punishment are not supported by scripture, we move on to other questions. The most prominent one is, "If there is no hell and eternal punishment, and if there is universal salvation, then what did Jesus accomplish on the cross?"

6

Christ's Work on the Cross

No One Church Doctrine

The synoptic gospels (Matthew, Mark, and Luke) record Jesus's ministry mainly taking place in Northern Israel—an area designated as Galilee. Near the end of Jesus's earthly ministry, he led his disciples to a place called Caesarea Philippi, in the Northeastern corner of Galilee. It is about as far from Jerusalem as Jesus and his group of disciples could get. Caesarea Philippi is a turning point in Jesus's ministry.

At Caesarea Philippi, Jesus asks his disciples, "Who do men say that I am?" (Matt 16:13; Mark 8:27; Luke 9:18). After the disciples convey the local gossip (e.g., that Jesus was John the Baptist reincarnated, Elijah who had returned, or some other ancient prophet) Jesus asks the disciples a more personal question. He asks, "Who do you say that I am?" The disciples are silent until Peter blurts out, "You are the Messiah, the Son of the living of God" (Matt 16:16; Mark 8:29; Luke 9:20). Matthew adds that Peter did not recognize who Jesus was on his own, but God had revealed this truth to him (Matt 16:17).

Once his identity was out in the open, Jesus begins to clarify for the disciples what being the Messiah means for him and for them. We might recall that the Jews were waiting for the Messiah. While they waited for the Messiah to appear, the envisioned that he would be a strong political figure who would overthrow the oppressive Roman government and establish God's kingdom with Israel as its center. James and John, the sons of Zebedee and members of the inner circle of the disciples, expressed this expectation when they asked Jesus to sit at his right hand and his left when he came into his kingdom (Matt 20:21; Mark 10:37). James and John make this request even though Jesus had already talked about his approaching death.

At Caesarea Philippi, Jesus first tells his disciples what must happen to the Son of Man, or Messiah. Mark writes, "Then he began to teach them that the Son of Man must undergo great suffering, and be rejected by the elders, the chief priests, and the scribes, and be killed, and after three days rise again" (Mark 8:31). Jesus' prediction is also recorded in Matthew 16:21 and Luke 9:22.

Shortly after his conversation with the disciples, Jesus takes Peter, James, and John with him up a mountain for a time of prayer. While they are on that mountain, the disciples witness Jesus's transfiguration. Peter, James, and John see Jesus in his glory, they observe him talking with Moses and Elijah, and they hear the voice of God proclaiming that Jesus is God's son and that they are to listen to him (Matt 17:1–8; Mark 9:2–8; Luke 9:28–36).

The four men come down from the mountain. After Jesus heals a boy with epilepsy, he leads his disciples south. Luke notes, "Jesus set his face toward Jerusalem" (Luke 9:51). Jesus senses the powerful forces, which had been set in motion by his teaching and his ministry. He could see his destiny.

While they travel toward Jerusalem, Jesus again tells his disciples what will happen to him. The gospel writers record Jesus's second prediction of his suffering and death (Matt 17:22–23; Mark 9:30–32; Luke 9:43–45). At this point, the disciples could be accused of selective listening. They don't want to wrestle with the idea that the Messiah might not come and overthrow the Roman government. Neither do they want to hear that their beloved leader would be tortured and executed.

Jesus and his disciples continue their journey to Jerusalem. As they draw nearer to Jerusalem, Jesus makes a third prediction of his death (Matt 20:17; Mark 10:32–34; Luke 18:31–34). Not wavering from what appears to be his destiny, Jesus enters Jerusalem. We commemorate this event as Palm Sunday, the first day of Holy Week. During his last week on earth, before he celebrates the Passover Meal with his disciples, Matthew records a fourth prediction by Jesus concerning his death. He says, "You know that after two days the Passover is coming, and the Son of Man will be handed over to be crucified" (Matt 26:2).

The gospel of John does not record Jesus's predictions of his suffering and death as the synoptic gospels do. John does have Jesus refer to his "glorification" frequently in Jesus's discourse with his disciples in John 12:17. At one point in his conversation, Jesus says, "The hour has come for the Son of Man to be glorified. Very truly, I tell you, unless a grain of wheat falls into the earth and dies, it remains just a single grain; but if it dies, it bears much fruit" (John 12:23–24).

Jesus predicts his torture and execution four times. Though the disciples don't appear to catch on to what Jesus is saying, the readers of these gospels understand that it is necessary for the Son of Man, God's Messiah, to suffer and die. Christians through the ages understood that it was necessary for Jesus to die. There is disagreement, though, about why Jesus needed to die. Jesus never gives us an answer.

There is no official, orthodox doctrine of atonement. It isn't like the doctrine of the trinity or our belief that Jesus was both human and divine. A universally accepted doctrine of atonement cannot be found in any of the creeds nor in any of the decrees from various church councils. We agree humankind's relationship with God was bruised and broken. It wasn't what God wanted it to be, nor what we wanted it to be. The purpose of Jesus's death and resurrection was to reconcile humankind with God. Several motifs have evolved around exactly how Jesus accomplished this. This is where there is discussion and disagreement.

It must be noted that the various motifs of atonement are not mutually exclusive. They are not "either/or" but can be "both/and." To believe in one motif of the atonement is not to deny the validity of other motifs. As followers of Jesus, it is possible for us to believe principally in one motif of the atonement and also appreciate aspects of other perspectives on the atonement.

PENAL SUBSTITUTIONARY MOTIF—
POPULAR BUT QUESTIONABLE

Sadly, the most popularly held theory of atonement, at this point in history, is the most theologically suspect. The theory is called the "penal substitutionary" theory. It goes something like this: In the beginning, Adam and Eve rebelled against God and disobeyed God. Sin entered the world and all of humanity. We can never escape or shed our sinfulness. Try as we might, we are never able to achieve perfection and attain sinlessness. Because of this we are doomed. The Scripture attests, "For the wages of sin is death" (Rom 6:23). Thankfully, Jesus shed his godliness, took on our form and became a human who was without sin. Sinless Jesus never needed to experience the price of sin. He never needed to die. Jesus did die, though. He was tortured and crucified. Jesus paid the price for our sinfulness. He died so that we would not need to die and so that we could experience new life.

In the 1960s Bill Bright, President of Campus Crusade for Christ, developed the "Four Spiritual Laws." Since then these spiritual laws have become foundational for many Christians' understanding of what a means to be a Christian. These laws are based on the penal substitutionary theory of atonement. They are:

1. God loves you and offers a wonderful plan for your life (John 3:16; 10:10).

2. Man is sinful and separated from God. Therefore, he cannot know and experience God's love and plan for his life (Rom 3:23; 6:23).

3. Jesus Christ is God's only provision for man's sin. Through him, you can know and experience God's love and plan for your life (Rom 5:8; 1 Cor 15:3—6; John 14:6).

4. We must individually receive Jesus Christ as Savior and Lord; then we can know and experience God's love and plan for our lives (John 1:12; 3:1—8; Eph 2:8—9; Rev 3:20). God loves you and offers a wonderful plan for your life (John 3:16; 10:10).[1]

Many people are uncomfortable with the penal substitutionary motif of the atonement, for several reasons. One of the main arguments against the motif is that it did not appear on the Christian theological scene until one thousand years after the life, death, and resurrection of Jesus. The early followers of The Way did not view Jesus's death and resurrection from this perspective. This motif of the atonement was developed by Anselm of Canterbury and can be seen in his 1098 work, *Cur Deus Homo* (Why a God-Man).[2] In this work, Anselm is ahead of his time in articulating a sense of justice.[3]

It is this sense of justice that holds so much appeal for us as we seek to comprehend Jesus's work on the Cross. We are people who are governed by laws, whose purpose is to create justice. The penal substitutionary motif brings the atonement "down-to-earth," places it in the context of our daily experience of do's/dont's—punishments/rewards. It also "lends itself to metaphors, allegories, and parables that appeal to us. For example, this old standby: A judge passes a sentence of death upon a criminal who deserves nothing less; the judge then stands, removes his robe, and goes to the electric chair in the criminal's stead."[4]

1. Bright, "Spiritual Laws."
2. Jones, *Better Atonement*, 381.
3. Jones, *Better Atonement*, 392.
4. Jones, *Better Atonement*, 392.

Though this illustration has often been spoken from a pulpit, it over-looks the obvious point that no criminal justice system would allow such an action to be accepted as justice. The penal substitutionary motif still empha-sizes God's anger over God's love. It reduces God's essence of love to one of God's characteristics. Anger and God's sense of justice become greater than God's core characteristic of love. Justice is achieved by Jesus's torture and execution.

This emphasis on God's anger and justice carries over to our individual lives as we seek to live out our faith. Our daily walk is in the shadow of God's anger and sense of justice rather than in the light of God's love and grace.

Stephen Copeland, in his book *Where the Colors Blend*, shares his ex-perience of living in the shadows and his pilgrimage into the light. Early in his book, he reflects on an incident when he and his friends experienced the harsh condemnation of other Christians. The group Stephen was with was participating in a church softball tournament to raise money for Christian missions in South America. They were doing this on Sunday afternoon. A pastor criticized them for breaking the Sabbath saying, "There's nothing Christian about you guys." Another Christian informed the group, "A ball is the devil's tool."[5]

Copeland shares his thoughts on the encounter.

> What a sad, sobering thing it is to think that Christians—pastors, even—build their entire lives upon the foundation of a god that is hardly enjoyable, one that, for example, doesn't permit church softball on Sundays. It seems to me that these types of gods are often used in an attempt to manipulate or control others. And, even though I can denounce this type of God in my head and in my writing, I wonder if this type of god—the finger-pointing, guilt-tripping god that doesn't want you to enjoy anything that isn't related to prayer, the Bible, or church—has corrupted my heart. Maybe the gods we so readily denounce are often the gods we are most likely to follow.[6]

A few pages later in his book, Copeland writes about his personal ex-perience of living in the shadows of God's anger and judgment.

> . . . This is my spirituality these days . . . I hardly enjoy it. In my past, I have claimed that I have found the secret to life and its meaning—God—and yet I metaphorically walk around hanging my head and hitting my leg over and over, as I did in so many golf tournaments in college. No, really, I remember walking up

5. Copeland, *Colors Blend*, 37, used with permission.
6. Copeland, *Colors Blend*, 37, used with permission.

the fairway or the rough (mostly the rough!), hanging my head and punching myself in the thigh over and over when I was playing poorly in tournaments.

Unworthiness.
Unworthiness because of my performance.

Unworthiness because my performance did not meet personal expectations . . . I am back in college, golfing again, walking up the fairway and bruising my thigh with my fist like a freaking psychopath! And what's worse is that I try to convince others to follow Christ, telling them that it will free them and bring them joy, when deep down I know that it has only bounded me in a cage of my lacking performance.[7]

The Holy Spirit was with Stephen Copeland in the midst of his struggles, though. The Spirit surround Copeland with a community of dedicated, self-sacrificing, and servant-minded missionaries and friends. They shared a similar upbringing and common faith. Most of them were older and more mature than Copeland. They had lived through triumphs and tragedies, and in both had experienced God's love and grace. The Spirit used their witness to touch Copeland's life and change his heart. A turning point occurs while Copeland is visiting the South American missions he has worked hard to support. On the last day of his visit, he and his friends visit Iguazzu Falls. Surrounded by the falls, Copeland hears the Spirit's voice. "*When you are filled with wonder and awe for the mysteries of life, you will always venture down the path. You will know no other way. Only the fearful or complacent turn back. Only the spiritually deaf and mystically blind will settle for a life of absolutes and solutions and formulas.*"[8]

Copeland is drenched by the water spray from the falls. He again hears the Spirit's voice.

What do you see and hear *and* feel *and* taste?"
"You!" My soul shouts. I *see* the falls and I *hear* the falls and I *feel* the falls and I can *taste* the falls! I am covered in the same water that tumbles down these cliffs. I am one with the most magnificent thing my body has ever seen and heard and tasted and felt!"
"*At the center of Us, the ethos of the Triune dance, is a love that is to be experienced—experienced by you. To be seen. To be heard. To be felt. To be tasted. Now close your eyes.*"

---

7. Copeland, *Colors Blend*, 39, used with permission.
8. Copeland, *Colors Blend*, 261, used with permission.

"Okay" my soul says, surrendering.

*"I baptize you in the name of the Trinity—the Father and the
Son and the Holy Spirit. Stand here as I drench you with my love
and grace. Taste the kiss of the divine on your lips. And when you
leave, do not forget that these waterfalls are only a metaphor for
what already is of life—a mystery full; of love and grace that is to
be experienced."*[9]

Criticism of the penal substitutionary motif continues. It replaces
God's love and acceptance with wrath and judgment. This is contradictory
to the image of God we see in the person of Jesus. The emphasis on justice
tempts us to focus on the keeping of the law, rather than to contemplate the
experience of God's grace in our daily lives. The penal substitutionary motif,
finally, makes the resurrection of Jesus Christ unnecessary.

The emphasis of the theory is on the cross—Jesus's torture and execution. Jesus paid the price. Jesus died so that we would not need to die; Jesus
died so that we might live. Once Jesus had done that; once he had become
the bridge to a new relationship with God, there was no need for anything
else. The resurrection continues to be a reality. We do not stop celebrating
the resurrection on Easter Sunday. (The candy and egg industries would rise
up in revolt!) The resurrection, though, becomes superfluous. Thankfully
there are other motifs we can consider.

RANSOM CAPTIVE MOTIF—THE LION,
THE WITCH, AND THE WARDROBE

A popular atonement theory during the first thousand years of Christianity
is called the Ransom Captive Motif. It is based on a verse in the gospel of
Mark. Jesus is speaking to James and John, who have just requested to sit on
his right and on his left hand—positions of power—when he establishes his
kingdom. Jesus tells James and John that striving for power and prestige is
something the Gentiles do, but not his disciples. To emphasize this truth,
Jesus points to himself and says, "For the Son of Man came not to be served
but to serve, and to give his life a ransom for many" (Mark 10:45). Ignoring
the fact that Jesus's words were meant to emphasize the necessity of service
in the lives of his followers, people focused on the word "ransom." Jesus'
death on the cross was a ransom.

The Ransom Captive motif of the atonement was popularized in modern times by C.S. Lewis in his book *The Lion, the Witch, and the Wardrobe.*

---

9. Copeland, *Colors Blend,* 262, used with permission.

In that book, mischievous, rebellious Edmund, one of the Pevensie children, falls captive to the White Witch. Through his love of Turkish Delight candy, he betrays his kindred, the messianic lion Aslan, and the subjects of Narnia. Edmund's actions result in his imprisonment. Edmund cannot return to his siblings nor is he free to serve Aslan the messianic lion. A greater punishment awaits Edmund, though. The ancient laws of Narnia also grant the White Witch the right to execute him.

We see Adam and Eve in Edmund. Edmund's love of Turkish Delight is similar to the attraction Eve and Adam have for the fruit of the Tree of the Knowledge of Good and Evil. As Edmund betrayed family, Narnians, and Aslan for the savory candy, so Adam and Eve bargained away the freedom of humankind to Satan. Since then, Satan has held sway over humankind. The pages of the Hebrew Scriptures bear witness to this.[10]

Aslan intervenes and strikes a bargain with the White Witch. He will take the place of Edmund and allow the White Witch to slaughter him on the great stone table. Aslan is alone, while the White Witch is surrounded by her minions. They cheer as she plunges her dagger into Aslan's heart.

The White Witch believes that she has won. She has gained the victory over Aslan and will to rule over Narnia forever. The White Witch, however, has misinterpreted the ancient laws of Narnia. Death cannot contain Aslan. He comes back to life. Not only has Aslan ransomed Edmund through his death, but the "very much alive" Aslan joins with the Narnians in their war against the White Witch and defeats her.

Aslan's actions on the great stone table are a metaphor of Jesus' work on the cross. Through his death on the cross, Jesus pays the price and ransoms humankind from their captor, Satan. Satan believes that he has won the battle and he will be able to rule forever. He underestimates God's power, though. The Holy Spirit breaths the breath of life back into Jesus's lifeless body. The stone is rolled away and on Easter morning the women and disciples discover an empty tomb. Later, the followers of Jesus encounter a living Jesus. They observe him ascend into heaven and sit at God's right hand. They are then filled with the Holy Spirit and are empowered to bear witness to the gospel of Jesus Christ to Jerusalem, Judea, Samaria, and the uttermost parts of the earth. Satan is defeated and God's kingdom is established on earth.

The Lion, the Witch and the Wardrobe is a popular and entertaining book. The Ransom Captive motif of atonement is appealing on several levels. There are, though, several arguments against it.

One point of opposition focuses on the presumption that Satan is in the position to bargain with God. Satan's genealogy is rather obscure. A

---

10. Jones, *Better Atonement*, 439.

popular train of thought is that Satan is a fallen angel. Satan was the great-est of God's created beings; second only to the Lord. Unfortunately, Satan became envious of God and dissatisfied with being second. Satan's envy inspired him to instigate a rebellion against God and he became the Lord's arch enemy. Much of this is based on a passage in Isaiah:

> How you are fallen from heaven,
> O Day Star, son of Dawn!
> How you are cut down to the ground,
> You who laid the nations low!
> You said in your heart,
> "I will ascend to heaven:
> I will raise my throne
> Above the stars of God;
> I will sit on the mount of assembly
> On the heights of Zaphon;
> I will ascend to the tops of the clouds,
> I will make myself like the Most High."
> But you are brought down to Sheol,
> To the depths of the Pit (Isa 14:12–15).

This passage, however, is about the King of Babylon. Any exegesis of the passage cannot link these words to any angelic, satanic, or demonic being.

Many see Satan in the early chapters of Genesis as the tempter, in the Garden of Eden, of Eve and Adam. The writer of Genesis, though, identifies Eve's tempter as a serpent. This is not a problem, many insist. Satan is a shapeshifter, like Minerva McGonagall and Sirius Black in the Harry Potter series. He assumed the form of a snake. Most biblical scholars reject that interpretation, however. The writer(s) of Genesis had Adam and Eve's arch-enemy as a snake because of humankind's natural aversion to snakes. Snakes are also easily associated with evil.

The word "satan," is usually translated "accuser" or "adversary." It is used to describe both human adversaries and also a supernatural being. The first time the word appears in the Hebrew Scriptures is in Num 22:22. An angel of the Lord is sent to stand in opposition to Balaam. The angel, who stands against Balaam as his adversary, is described as "satan." When the definite article is attached to the word, it denotes a supernatural being. This is first seen in the book of Job. The heavenly being, Satan, is portrayed as an accuser of Job and also as a being who does God's bidding. In Zechariah's vision (Zech 3:1–7) Satan is seen as the adversary or prosecutor of the na-tion of Israel. The Lord rebukes Satan, in this vision, and forgives Israel.

Nowhere in the Hebrew Scriptures is Satan viewed as a being who can hold people captive. Nowhere is Satan understood as an opponent with whom God must bargain.

In the New Testament, Satan is seen as a tempter of Jesus in the three synoptic gospels (Matthew, Mark, and Luke). In the first letter attributed to Peter, Satan is pictured as a lion seeking to devour earnest and faithful Christians (1 Pet 5:8). It is in the apocalyptic vision of the Book of Revelation, where Satan is described as God's adversary in the classic battle between good and evil. Jesus refuses to bargain with Satan in the temptation stories. In the other portrayals of Satan, he is not any being with whom God would wish to bargain. God has no need to bargain with Satan.

The specific role of a person who seeks to serve as a redeemer (go el) is described and portrayed in the Hebrew Scriptures. "The kinsman-redeemer is a male relative who, according to various laws of the Pentateuch, had the privilege or responsibility to act on behalf of a relative who was in trouble, danger . . . The term designates one who delivers or rescues (Gen 48:16) or redeems property or person (Lev 27:9–25, 25:47–55).[11] Boaz acts as the kinsman-redeemer in the book of Ruth. Throughout the history of Israel, the Lord takes on the role of the nation's redeemer. The Lord is both Father and Deliverer (Exodus 20:2). God also acts as rescuer of the weak and needy (Psalm 82:4; Daniel 6:27; Jeremiah 20:13) and preserver of the sheep of Israel (Ezekiel 34:10–12, 22).[12]

The Lord, though, is not confined to act a certain way. God cannot be restrained by the expectations placed on the role of kinsman-redeemer. God's actions, through Jesus's death on the cross, can be interpreted as the ransom paid by the kinsman-redeemer. God, however, breaks out of the role of kinsman-redeemer. Beyond the payment of death, God brings forth new life. Death cannot vanquish God.

Even though there are significant arguments against the Ransom Captive motif of the atonement, this view of Jesus' salvific work was helpful to Christians in the first millennia of the church. This atonement motif can still be meaningful to Christians today.

Two years ago Stephen Abernathy received a heart transplant. Stephen had suffered from cardiomyopathy for a decade. During those ten years, his lifestyle slowly deteriorated, even though Stephen was resolute in observing his dietary and exercise regimens. Near the end, Stephen was confined to his

11. Got Questions, "Kinsman Redeemer."
12. Got Questions, "Kinsman Redeemer."

home. He could barely catch his breath. His body was bloated with excess fluid. Blood clots were a constant threat and Stephen was always exhausted. Stephen knew that he was near death and his quality of life had deteriorated to such an extent that he was almost welcoming death's arrival.

Everything changed the afternoon that Stephen received a phone call that a donor match had been found. He was rushed to the hospital. Within hours, Stephen was prepped for surgery. Once he recovered from his surgery and finished rehabilitation, Stephen felt like a new man. He had been given new life.

Stephen was well aware that someone had died so that he could live. In his case, a sixteen-year-old boy had lost control of his car and crashed after a late-night party. There were six young people in the car, but the driver was the only fatality.

Stephen's children were all in their twenties. He still remembered, though, the sleepless nights his wife and he endured as they worried and waited for their children to come home from parties and dates during their children's teen years. They had experienced the common fear of parents— receiving a late-night phone call informing them an accident had occurred. Stephen could only imagine the depth of grief and the pain felt by the young man's parents and family. He hoped the parents found some meaning, purpose, and comfort in their son's death by allowing him to become an organ donor.

The cost of his new life and health, which had been paid for by others, often crossed Stephen's mind. He knew the life he now lived was a very costly gift. As a Christian, Stephen likened what happened to him physically with what occurred with him spiritually. A sixteen-year-old boy had died and had set Stephen free from the prison created by his heart condition. Similarly, Jesus had paid the price through his death and resurrection to set Stephen free and restore his relationship with God. The price had been paid; Stephen had been redeemed.

CHRISTUS VICTOR MOTIF—VICTORY OVER SIN, DEATH, AND THE DEVIL

Another forgotten atonement belief of the early church is the Christus Victor motif. Sidelined for almost one thousand years, the theory was revived in the early twentieth century by a Swedish bishop, Gustaf Aulen. The bishop accomplished this feat with the publication of his book, *Christus Victor: An Historical Study of the Three Main Types of the Atonement*. Aulen contends that not only was the Christus Victor motif widely held in the early church, but it was also the theory held by most of the church fathers. Anselm was critical of this theory in his work, and the idea that Jesus provided humankind with victory over sin, death, and the devil, was surpassed by the idea that Jesus died for our sins.[13]

Aulen contends that the early church did not understand Jesus's death on the cross as a payment for the sins of humankind. "Instead, Christ's death is God's victory over sin and death. God conquers death by fully entering into it. God conquers Satan by using the very means employed by the Evil One. Thus, the crucifixion is not a necessary transaction to appease a wrathful and justice-demanding deity, but an act of divine love.[14]

The highlight of Jesus's death and resurrection was not the satisfaction of God's wrath—as in the penal substitutionary theory—but rather the demonstration of the depth of God's love and the power of that love. Sin was overcome by the power of love and forgiveness with the admonition to "go and sin no more" (John 8:11). Even the reoccurrence of sin is overcome by an unlimited supply of love and forgiveness.

In the resurrection of Jesus, God's divine love overcomes death. Paul discusses death and the resurrection of the dead in his letter to the Corinthians. He writes, "When this perishable body puts on imperishability, and this mortal body puts on immortality, then the saying that is written will be fulfilled: 'Death has been swallowed up in victory.' 'Where, O death, is your victory? Where, O death, is your sting?' " (1 Cor 15:54–55). Physical death is no longer "the end." There is mortality and immortality. Humankind has the promise and hope of new life, because of the power of God's love. Until that time of our physical death, Paul stresses that followers of Jesus live a new life on earth because we have died at the time of our baptism. To the Christians in Rome Paul writes, "   Do you not know that all of us who have been baptized into Christ Jesus were baptized into his death? Therefore we have been buried with him by baptism into death, so that, just as Christ was raised from the dead by the glory of the Father, so we too might walk in newness of life" (Rom 6:3–4). Walking in the light of God's love, we walk in new life. The fear of death has been overcome because perfect love casts out fear (1 John 4:8).

The Evil One, the one who lies, tempts, and seeks to devour, has been overcome and defeated by God's love in the death and resurrection of Jesus. God's love empowers humankind. Men and women are free to love rather than to hate, to accept rather than to judge, to serve rather than to be served. "God entered fully into the bondage of death, turned it inside out by making

13. Jones, *Better Atonement*, 456.
14. Boyd, "The Christus Victor."

it a moment of victory, and thereby liberates humanity to live lives of love without the fear of death"[15]

The Christus Victor motif of the atonement sees beyond the cruelty and ugliness of the crucifixion and beholds the beauty of God's love. The love that is seen is the love that transforms individual lives and the world.

Lamar Jenkins relaxed on a lounge chair in his backyard patio. His three grandchildren were playing in the pool. Watching them play and splash in the pool and hearing their laughter and giggles brought joy to his heart. The scene also reminded Lamar of how close he came to losing it all.

Fifteen years ago, Lamar's world was about to come crashing down upon him. He was on the verge of losing his job. Lamar's wife of twenty years was threatening to leave him, and his two children would have nothing to do with him. He lived a lonely existence with a bottle of vodka—his preferred beverage—his only companion. The bottle not only deadened his pain, which he denied having, it also blinded him to the effects of his drinking. Lamar thought he was living a normal, somewhat successful, middle-class life.

In desperation and at wit's end at how to save her family, Lamar's wife arranged for an intervention. She arranged for Lamar's supervisor and a co-worker to participate in the intervention along with her son and daughter, a couple with whom she and Lamar were friends, and the family's pastor. One Saturday morning she convinced Lamar to accompany her and gather ideas for remodeling their bathroom—a project they had talked about for many months. When they returned home, they found the group gathered in their living room. The pastor greeted Lamar and before he got over his surprise, the pastor asked him to sit down.

Tearfully, Lamar's wife began to explain why she had called the meeting. Lamar wanted to bolt; to run for the door, but something kept him glued to his chair. One by one, the people closest to him told Lamar what his drinking had done. Lamar listened. He wanted to object, but he was told to remain quiet. Their words stung. Those same words also began to seep into his heart. Lamar began to weep when his wife described how the alcohol had changed him and he was not the man she married. When his sixteen-year-old daughter told him that she missed her daddy and wanted him back, Lamar broke down. He had had no idea of the pain and suffering his drinking had been causing. After everyone had shared their stories, the pastor offered to drive Lamar to a rehabilitation facility. A suitcase had already been packed for him.

15. Jones, *Better Atonement*, 477.

The thirty days in the rehabilitation facility had been tough—they had also been life-giving. Lamar had to face the issues he had been trying to cover up—and to run from—by his drinking. The group leader and his fellow group members shared that he needed to place his faith in a higher power—he needed to let go and let God. When Lamar did let go, he fell into God's arms and was embraced by God's love. It was in his relationship with that higher power and in his letting go of all that he was trying to hide and control that Lamar found the strength and ability to turn away from his drinking. As Jesus was victorious in his life, death, and resurrection, so Lamar was victorious in breaking free from the chains that entrapped him. God's love, in the person of the Holy Spirit, gave him the power to live an alcohol-free life.

Lamar was religious in attending weekly AA meetings. They had been a vital part of his life for fifteen years. Those years had not all been easy. Lamar had to earn the respect of his superiors at work. He had to rekindle the flames of passion and love in his relationship with his wife, and he had to repair his relationship with his son and daughter. There were times when he began to imagine it would be so much easier if he only had a drink. A few times he almost fell off the wagon. Those were times when the Spirit would remind Lamar of the depth and steadfastness of God's love for him. His sponsor, family, and friends would surround and support him with their love. Lamar would be given the strength to continue to be victorious in this area of his life.

As Lamar sat and watched the antics of his grandchildren, heard their laughter, and saw their smiles, he was overwhelmed by God's love. Not only was it so deep that it drove God to experience the totality of humankind's existence—even death—it was also steadfast enough to stay with Lamar in his inebriation and his sobriety. God's love was unwavering in his life.

Unlike Lamar, Bonita Juarez had never tasted an alcoholic beverage. Still, she struggled. As a Latina, Bonita was a member of a small minority in her high school. That small minority marked her. She was bullied by a few of her classmates who felt she should go back to where she belonged. If they knew, these bullies chose to ignore the fact that Bonita had been born in the United States. Other classmates avoided her and the other Latinos, simply because they were different. Even though it was the twenty-first century, open-mindedness and acceptance were not strong points of either her high school or the community in which she lived.

The challenges that Bonita faced didn't stop there. Bonita's name could be translated "pretty." Bonita did not feel pretty, though. She believed what many people told her, or implied—she was ugly. Bonita wore glasses to correct her nearsightedness. In a school where contact lenses were the norm, glasses were ridiculed. Bonita was also chubby. In a world where thinness and fitness were valued, being chubby was not cool; rather, it was the object of social shunning. Bonita felt very much alone in the crowded halls of her school.

Bonita's response to the attitudes and comments of the people around her was to internalize them. She didn't stand up to them and neither did she fight them. She believed them and began to echo those comments in her thoughts. "Being Latina was bad," she told herself. None of the people she wished she could be wore glasses. She was fat! She was ugly! She was worthless! Bonita became increasingly angry at her situation and herself. She expressed her anger by cutting herself. Bonita would repeat the litany of put-downs and criticisms as she drew the edge of the razor blade across her skin. There would be pain and blood, and for some reason, it felt good. To keep her cutting a secret, Bonita always wore long sleeves and slacks no matter how hot it might be.

Bonita was in a prison—one that was not made with bars, but rather with the comments and attitudes of others. They provided a never-ending chorus in Bonita's mind. She could not escape them. Neither could Bonita stop cutting herself. In fact, it became more frequent and longer in duration. The voices added a new refrain to their chorus—"You don't deserve to live." Bonita began to think about killing herself.

It had been a particularly bad day at school. Bonita had immediately gone to her room when she arrived home so she could express her anger and cut herself. In her haste, she did not close her bedroom door completely. As she drew the blade of the razor down her arm, her mother barged into her room with a load of freshly laundered clothes. When she saw what her daughter was doing, she dropped the clothes, grabbed the razor blade out of Bonita's hand, and covered Bonita with a loving embrace.

The journey to quiet the voices in Bonita's head and build up her self-esteem was long and arduous. It involved therapists, medical doctors, and ongoing group sessions. Once Bonita's family understood the destructive nature of the comments and attitudes, they amended their behavior and rallied around Bonita. Bonita also elected to work with a spiritual counselor.

It was during her conversations with her spiritual counselor that Bonita learned about Jesus healing a woman who had been hemorrhaging for twelve years (Luke 8:42–48). The woman had been a social outcast—a person who was considered "unclean." Because of her unclean condition, the woman was prevented from worshiping her Lord. The woman touched the hem of Jesus's garment and was healed.

Bonita also read the story of the Gerasene demoniac (Mark 5:1-20). The man, who was possessed by evil spirits, was a danger to himself and others. He had been cast off by the people of his hometown and forced to live among the tombs—an unclean area. Though he was a Gentile and not considered one of God's chosen people, Jesus had confronted the man and cast out the evil spirits from him. Jesus had given the man a new life.

The love of God and the power of that love, which culminated in Jesus's death and resurrection, touched Bonita's heart. She was overwhelmed by God's love and empowered by that love to silence the voices and hear God's words of affirmation. Walking each day in that love and its power gave Bonita the ability to live a new life.

THE IMAGE OF LOVE MOTIF—ABELARD AND THE GREATEST EXAMPLE OF LOVE

The first converts to the Christian faith were not responding to any of the atonement motifs we have discussed. Later in their journeys of faith, they may have understood Jesus as one who ransomed them from Satan's claims upon their lives. They may have glimpsed the power over sin, death, and the devil, which Jesus won for them on the cross. Their primary reason for entering the fellowship of believers, though, was their perception that Jesus, through his life, death, and resurrection, had ushered God's kingdom into the world. This kingdom was diametrically opposed to the political and religious institutions they experienced daily. Those kingdoms were based on power, control, the exultation of self, and the judgment of others deemed unworthy or different. God's kingdom was based on God's love, and grace, and the understanding that all people were God's children. Jesus not only opened God's kingdom to all of humankind, but Jesus was also the greatest example of what life in God's kingdom was like.

Throughout the Hebrew Scriptures, God is seen inviting God's people into a loving relationship with God and with each other. This was God's intention when God spoke to Abraham and invited him and his wife Sarah to journey to the land God would give them. God longed for a relationship with the descendants of Abraham when God called Moses to lead them out of slavery in Egypt and into the Promised Land. God gave the Law to the Israelites so that they might practice and experience God's love and grace in their relationships with each other and in their relationship with God. The temple system and the prophets were used by God to call God's people into a relationship of love and grace. The culmination of God's acts of invitation was the life, death, and resurrection of Jesus.

When Jesus began his ministry, he proclaimed to the people around him, "The time is fulfilled, and the kingdom of God has come near; repent, and believe in the good news" (Mark 1:15). The word "repent" is often understood to mean confess all of your sins and ask God's forgiveness. The Greek word literally means to change one's mind, though. Instead of confessing one's sins, Jesus' invitation could be understood to mean "to see things from a new perspective." From this new perspective, Jesus invites people to see that the kingdom of God has arrived. People are then invited to believe—to live in the reality of God's kingdom—to love and to forgive freely. (Thus, they abandon the self-centered, power-grabbing activities of the present age and their previous lives.)

The writers of the New Testament were concerned that love is the centerpiece of the lives of the first Christians. They frequently exhorted the followers of Jesus to love. The writer of John's gospel records Jesus's discourse with his disciples in the last days of his life. Preparing them for his departure, Jesus says, "I give you a new commandment, that you love one another. Just as I have loved you, you also should love one another" (John 13:34). The apostle Paul writes to a contentious church in Corinth that is obsessed with the demonstration of the Holy Spirit's gifts and reminds them, "If I have prophetic powers, and understand all mysteries and all knowledge, and if I have all faith, so as to remove mountains, but do not have love, I am nothing" (1 Cor 13:2). Paul goes on to say, "Now faith, hope, and love abide, these three; and the greatest of these is love" (1 Corinthians 13:7). The writer of the first letter of John instructs his readers that "Whoever says, "I am in the light," while hating a brother or sister, is still in the darkness. Whoever loves a brother or sister lives in the light, and in such a person there is no cause for stumbling" (1 John 2:9–10).

Jesus's life and ministry were examples of the love God had for humankind and the kind of love God invited people to have for each other. Healing a leper and forgiving a woman caught in adultery were expressions of kingdom love. Dining with tax collectors, responding to a Roman Centurion's request to heal his servant, and casting out a legion of evil spirits from a tormented man demonstrated the depth and expanse of God's love for God's creation. The greatest expression of God's love, however, was the death and resurrection of Jesus, the Son of God. The writer of John's gospel proclaims, "For God so loved the world that he gave his only Son, so that everyone who believes in him may not perish but may have eternal life. Indeed, God did not send the Son into the world to condemn the world, but in order that the world might be saved through him" (John 3:16–17).

The early church fathers picked up on the proclamation of the New Testament writers and echoed their claim that the cross and resurrection was the ultimate example of God's love for humankind. Their thoughts can be read in some of the earliest Christian writings such as, "*Epistle to Diogentus*, the *Shepherd of Hermas*, and the letters of Clement of Rome, Ignatius of Antioch, Clement of Alexandria, Hippolytus of Rome, and the *Martyrdom of Polycarp*."[16]

The Image of Love Motif was taken up in the Middle Ages by Peter Abelard (1078–1142), a brilliant philosopher and theologian. Abelard rejected Augustine's teaching on original sin, arguing that, though humankind is inclined toward sin because of Adam, we cannot be held accountable for his sin. If humankind cannot be held liable for each other's sins, neither can a person arrange for the absolution of another's sin. In Abelard's view, Jesus could not have died on the cross to absolve humankind of sin. Instead, "Christ's death serves as an example that beckons us to lives of sacrificial love."[17]

Many argue against Abelard, saying that the Image of Love Motif downplays the crucifixion. Jesus's crucifixion wasn't necessary, they point out, if it was only a further example of God's love and the type of love God wants all of humankind to exhibit in our lives.

Binh was a refugee from Viet Nam. He immigrated to the United States in 1975 with his wife and three children. The family was sponsored by a Lutheran congregation in Wisconsin. The congregation found housing for Binh's family, provided food and clothing, and even found Binh a job. Through the help of the congregation and his hard work, Binh was eventually able to start his own business. Through the years, he made his business into a very profitable enterprise. It paid for the college education of his three children and allowed his wife and him to live in an upscale area of town.

The witness of the people of the congregation left a lasting impression on Binh and his family. They had never experienced such great love. The family began to attend the congregation's worship services and learn about the Christian faith. The family read the Bible together and were taught what Jesus accomplished on the cross. They were amazed and overwhelmed by the degree of love demonstrated by Jesus. Two years later, on the anniversary of his immigration to the United States, Binh and his family were baptized into the Christian faith.

16. Jones, *Better Atonement*, 487.
17. Jones, *Better Atonement*, 509.

Forty years later Binh read about the plight of refugees from Latin America. He listened to the nightly news as the commentators described how children were separated from their parents and kept in cages. Binh saw pictures of the squalid conditions of the overcrowded refugee centers. Inspired by God's love, Binh decided to do something. He and his wife gave generously to the Christian organizations who were ministering to the needs of the refugees. Binh also decided to travel to the Southern border of the United States and volunteered to help the refugees in any way that he could. After all, loving and serving one another were what the cross of Christ and the kingdom of God were all about.

LOVE AND LIFE—TRANSFORMATIONAL ATONEMENT

There are several more atonement motifs. Some motifs focus on specific aspects of the ideas that have already been mentioned. Others combine elements of the different motifs. Still others offer unique perspectives. René Girard, an anthropologist and literary critic, interprets the atonement in the light of the Hebrew Scriptures scapegoat (Lev 16:21–22).[18] Stephen Burnhope views the cross and resurrection of Jesus through the lens of the covenants God made with Abraham and Moses.[19]

With the plethora of atonement motifs before us, we can become engrossed in analyzing them. We focus our attention on determining which one we agree with, or which one we believe is the most accurate. One important fact escapes our notice. The cross and resurrection of Jesus are not merely to be analyzed—they are to be experienced.

In the prologue to John's gospel (1:1–18), God's incarnation in the life and ministry of Jesus was one of life, light, grace, and truth. Later in the gospel, John adds that Jesus was an expression of God's love (John 3:16). Evidently, humankind does not handle light, life, grace, truth, and love very well, though. We rejected them and crucified Jesus. In light of God's action and our reaction, the cross and resurrection of Jesus proclaim an important truth. They announce that, "God simply won't rest until God has restored us, redeemed us, created *at-one-ment* with us."[20]

Stephen, Lamar, Bonita, and Binh discovered this truth. It changed their lives. They were not transformed by the threat of hell and eternal punishment. Rather, God's steadfast love and overwhelming grace accomplished that feat. Paul affirms God's determination when he writes,

18. Girard, *The Scapegoat*.

19. Burnhope, *New Perspective*.

20. Lose, *Making Sense*, 1739.

What then are we to say about these things? If God is for us, who is against us? He who did not withhold his own Son, but gave him up for all of us, will he not with him also give us everything else? Who will bring any charge against God's elect? It is God who justifies. Who is to condemn? It is Christ Jesus, who died, yes, who was raised, who is at the right hand of God, who indeed intercedes for us. Who will separate us from the love of Christ? Will hardship, or distress, or persecution, or famine, or nakedness, or peril, or sword? As it is written,

"For your sake we are being killed all day long; we are accounted as sheep to be slaughtered."

No, in all these things we are more than conquerors through him who loved us. For I am convinced that neither death, nor life, nor angels, nor rulers, nor things present, nor things to come, nor powers, nor height, nor depth, nor anything else in all creation, will be able to separate us from the love of God in Christ Jesus our Lord (Rom 8:31–39).

God's love, as it is expressed in Jesus's crucifixion and resurrection, sets us free. We are free to love, to forgive and to minister to the needs of others. The Holy Spirit moves in our freedom and empowers us to pattern our lives after Jesus.

7

Breaking Down the Barriers

The Benefits of a Hell-less World

The pharmaceutical companies have discovered the power of advertising prescription drugs. Every night television watchers are offered a cornucopia of miracle medications. After touting the wonders of their drugs for almost 30 or 60 seconds, a voice comes on to list the possible side effects. Usually, the voice is subdued, lower in volume, and speaks at such a fast rate that it is difficult to understand. Still, the listener comprehends the message. There are many side effects to the particular medication, and death is possible. One begins to wonder why any sane person would consider using such a potentially dangerous drug. Clearly, in the minds of many people, the benefits outweigh the risks. On their next visit to their doctor, they will suggest the drug become a part of their treatment program. These same people, during their visit with their doctor, will think to themselves, "*Other people will need to deal with the side effects, but I won't be affected.*" Not unlike these miracle medications, hell and the threat of eternal punishment have some serious side effects.

HELL SEPARATED—THE SAVED/ UNSAVED AND THE GOOD/BAD

Hell and the possible experience of God's wrath have been a blessing to the church. The church has effectively used Hell and the threat of eternal punishment to control its members and achieve its goals. Billions of dollars have been raised, for worthy projects, from parishioners in order to escape condemnation or to help relatives gain an early pardon from their sufferings. The church has been able to erect a façade of "One Lord, One Faith, One Baptism." People have been forced to give assent to theological doctrines— not because they believe them to be true, but because they fear punishment if they think the teachings to be false. The church and its doctrine of hell and eternal punishment have been a powerful force in creating and shaping societies and cultures. There are many other great accomplishments, which have been achieved through the use of the doctrine of hell and condemnation. There are also some significant side effects. One side effect is that the concept of hell does not unify. It divides, and division causes conflict.

Eddie and Lynn grew up in the 1950s. They were cousins, a year apart in age and living in neighboring towns. Several times a year they and their mothers would take bus trips to each other's home and spend the day together. Those days were filled with a great deal of laughter and adventure. There was one problem, though. Eddie was Lutheran and Lynn was Roman Catholic.

Lynn's mother had grown up in the Lutheran Church but had fallen in love and had married a Roman Catholic boy. To have the marriage take place in the Roman Catholic Church, Lynn's mother had promised to allow her children to be raised as a Roman Catholic. While Lynn attended worship services and various classes, she learned that Lutherans were outside the Church and, because of this, were not able to experience God's saving grace. In other words, Lutherans were condemned to hell and an eternity spent separated from God.

Eddie and his parents frequently attended Lutheran worship services and Eddie earned several 100% attendance awards for Sunday school. In his classes and during worship, Eddie was told that Roman Catholics relied on something called "works righteousness" rather than God's grace. Roman Catholics did good works to please God and win their salvation. Works righteousness, however, was condemned by Martin Luther. He argued that trying to earn one's salvation was a useless effort. Men and women could only rely on God's love and grace, which was given to them through the cross and resurrection of Jesus. Relying on works to gain salvation actually sentenced the person to an eternity in Hell.

Eddie and Lynn grew up together and played together, all the while being told that the other was lost for eternity. It didn't make sense to either of them. On the one hand, they were cousins who liked each other and played well together. On the other hand, they were the Saved and the Damned. Though this didn't create conflict between them—they left that to the adults—it did cause a division. Rather than being able to celebrate that they were God's children, they reminded each other that one was Lutheran and the other was Roman Catholic.

Kiersten was a teenager actively involved in her Episcopal congregation. She was president of the youth group and served as the youth representative on the congregational governing board. During the past two summers, Kiersten participated in two mission trips that were offered by her congregation. One of the mission trips was to Mexico, where her group participated in a Habitat for Humanity home build. The other trip was to a Navajo nation where she helped lead a Vacation Bible School experience for the children.

While searching through a website for Christian teenagers, Kiersten spotted an advertisement for a seminar on discipleship. Several hundred youths would descend upon a college campus on the east coast for a week-long focus on living as followers of Jesus. Kiersten's interest was piqued. She registered for the seminar and approached her congregation to sponsor her with a scholarship. Her congregation supported her by funding not only the registration costs but also the transportation expenses. The parish priest did caution her that the event was more toward the evangelical spectrum of the Christian family, rather than the Episcopal. The headline speakers were nationally known and reputable, so she affirmed that she thought it would be a positive experience for Kiersten.

Kiersten's excitement grew as she flew to the event. After deplaning and grabbing her bag from the baggage carousel, she boarded a shuttle for the college. Several other teens that were attending the seminar boarded the shuttle with her. Soon the van was filled with conversation as the teens shared where they were from and started the process of building relationships with each other.

The college was a Christian liberal arts college. Its campus was small, and it was easy for Kiersten to register and find her dorm room. When she opened the door, Kiersten discovered that her roommate was already there. As Kiersten unpacked, the two briefly shared their life stories. Kiersten discovered that her roommate was named Dee and her father was the pastor of a large, non-denominational congregation in Florida. Dee had two siblings—an older brother and a younger sister. She had accepted Jesus as her Lord and Savior when she was young and was baptized when she was only eight-years-old.

Dee was curious about Kiersten's family and church experience. Kiersten shared that she had a younger sister, too. When Kiersten told Dee she was a member of an Episcopal congregation, Dee furrowed her brow. Kiersten, ignoring Dee's concerned look, continued to tell Dee about her involvement in her congregation.

"You've never accepted Jesus as your Lord and Savior? You're not born again?" Dee questioned when Kiersten paused.

"No," Kiersten responded. I never had to accept Jesus as my Savior. The important thing is that he has accepted me as his child. I was born from above, when I was baptized a couple of weeks after I was born."

"It doesn't work that way," Dee informed Kiersten. "You must personally accept Jesus as your Lord and Savior and pray the sinner's prayer. The Bible says that you must first believe and then be baptized. If you don't repent and believe, you're lost. You will be condemned to hell and eternal punishment."

"It's fine for you to believe that," assured Kiersten. "But don't worry about me. I am quite sure that God loves me and holds me in God's hands."

Dee was going to continue the discussion, but the two girls realized that they needed to head toward the cafeteria for dinner and then attend the evening gathering.

Kiersten quickly discovered that the majority of seminar participants were from conservative evangelical or Pentecostal congregations. As she was learning the theological background of the other teens, they were learning about hers. Soon most of the other attendees knew that Kiersten had not received Jesus Christ as her Lord and Savior and had not been born again. Well-meaning young people that they were, they decided that before the end of the seminar they would convert Kiersten and convince her to ask Jesus to enter her life.

The plenary sessions were stimulating and the small group discussions were lively and thought-provoking. Kiersten felt that she was learning a lot that she could not only apply to her life but share with the other youths in her church group back home. Every night, however, Kiersten had to sit through mini inquisitions during which various participants shared Bible verses with her and attempted to convince her that she really wasn't a Christian and needed to become one.

Kiersten held her ground. She realized the other youth were not trying to be mean but were acting out of Christian concern for her eternal destiny, as they had been taught. She shared her faith story with them and affirmed her relationship with Jesus. It wasn't enough for the others. She hadn't repeated the magic words and, as far as they were concerned, she was going to Hell. At the end of the conference, having failed to convert Kiersten, her new friends assured her that they would continue to pray for her.

Reflecting on her experience, Kiersten believed the seminar had been positive and had provided her with an opportunity to grow in her faith. She was saddened, though, that she never was able to feel fully accepted by the other teens. She was different because she identified herself as an Episcopal Christian and because she didn't agree with the need to accept Jesus. An opportunity to celebrate God's love and grace, and together discover how to live out their faith as disciples of Jesus, had been marred by the division caused by hell and the threat of an eternity of experiencing God's wrath.

Eddie, Lynn, and Kiersten's stories are not isolated, nor are they exceptional. Such interactions are common and have been experienced by millions, and perhaps billions, of people throughout two millennia of the Christian Church. People are divided into groups. There were the righteous and the unrighteous, the good and the evil, the "in" and the "out," the "us" and the "them." Some of the encounters were benign, like Eddie and Lynn's. Two children, who were aware of the prejudices of adults but did not allow it to affect their playtime. Kiersten's conversations at the seminar, though judgmental and divisive, were at least the expression of a loving, but misguided, concern for her eternal salvation.

Other encounters have been the product of sadistic imaginations. The church father Tertullian, applied a measure of judgment—who would go to hell and who would not—based on whether or not they agreed with him. "Tertullian fantasized that not only the wicked would be in hell but also every philosopher and theologian who ever argued with him! He envisioned a time when he would look down from heaven at those people in hell and laugh with glee!"[1]

The pain and suffering that hell and its eternal condemnation were to exert in the afterlife all too often spilled over into the religious bigotry and hate campaigns of history. Augustine was not only one of the primary champions of hell but also of this kind of intolerance.

> [Augustine] was the first in the long line of Christian persecutors, and illustrates the character of the theology that swayed him in the wicked spirit that impelled him to advocate the right to persecute Christians who differ from those in power. The dark pages that bear the record of subsequent centuries are a damning witness to the cruel spirit that actuated Christians,

1. Vincent, "Salvation Conspiracy."

and the cruel theology that impelled it. Augustine was the first and ablest asserter of the principle which led to the Albigensian crusades, the Spanish armadas, Netherland's butcheries, the St. Bartholomew massacres, the accursed infamies of the Inquisition, the vile espionage, the hideous bale fires of Seville and Smithfield, the racks, the gibbets, the thumbscrews, and the subterranean torture-chambers used by churchly torturers.[2]

Several centuries after Augustine, the great reformer Martin Luther proclaimed the love and grace of God given to humankind through the cross and resurrection of Jesus. The gift of God's love and grace, according to Luther, was transformational in the Christian's life of faith. Luther writes:

> Faith is a living, bold trust in God's grace, so certain of God's favor that it would risk death a thousand times trusting in it. Such confidence and knowledge of God's grace makes you happy, joyful and bold in your relationship to God and all creatures. The Holy Spirit makes this happen through faith. Because of it, you freely, willingly and joyfully do good to everyone, serve everyone, suffer all kinds of things, love and praise the God who has shown you such grace.[3]

Luther recaptured the essence of Paul's message: "For by grace [we] have been saved through faith, and this is not [our] own doing; it is the gift of God—not the result of works, so that no one may boast. For we are what he has made us, created in Christ Jesus for good works . . ." (Eph 2:8–10a). He broke away from the church's emphasis on God's wrath and judgment and instead stressed God's love. In Luther's teaching of the priesthood of all believers, strides were made to replace the elitism of the Roman Catholic Church and European society with the egalitarianism of the early Christians. Paul reflected this idea when he exclaimed, "There is no longer Jew or Greek, there is no longer slave or free, there is no longer male and female; for all of you are one in Christ Jesus" (Gal 3:28).

At the same time, there appear to be limits to the unity Luther found in Christ. Luther's polemics against the pope and the Muslims reflected a hint of hell's condemnation. Luther called them both the antichrist—the one who stands against Christ, who would lead people in rebellion against God and, as a result, lead them to their eternal death (1 John 4:3; Rev 13:1–10). He said, "Antichrist is the pope and the Turk [Muslim] together. A beast full

---

2. Farrar, *Lives of the Fathers*, 253.
3. Luther, "An Introduction," 124.

of life must have a body and soul. The spirit or soul of Antichrist is the pope, his flesh or body the Turk."[4]

At the end of his life, Luther also expressed similar hostile feelings and thoughts toward the Jews. When the Reformation began, Luther was sympathetic to the Jewish resistance to the Roman Catholic Church. Luther thought the Jews would be attracted to the gospel (which focused on God's love and grace rather than the need to avoid God's wrath through good works), and convert to Christianity. When this did not happen in any measurable manner, he turned against the Jews. In 1543, near the end of his life, Luther wrote a book entitled *The Jews and Their Lies*.[5] Luther writes:

> I brief, dear princes and lords, those of you who have Jews under your rule if my counsel does not please you find better advice, so that you and we all can be rid of the unbearable, devilish burden of the Jews, lest we become guilty sharers before God in the lies, blasphemy, the defamation, and the curses which the mad Jews indulge in so freely and wantonly against the person of our Lord Jesus Christ, this dear mother, all Christians, all authority, and ourselves. Do not grant them protection, safe conduct, or communion with us. . . . With this faithful counsel and warning I wish to cleanse and exonerate my conscience.[6]

Luther's words have been blamed for the atrocities imposed upon the Jews by the Nazis in the 1930s and 1940s. While the degree of this influence is a hotly debated topic, Luther cannot be completely exonerated from his words. Luther and other Reformers made great strides in recapturing the love and grace of God in the message of Jesus' life and words. Still, they operated under the divisions of their time in history. God's love was tempered with hell's divisions of righteous/unrighteous, good/bad, and us/them. These divisions of hell clash with the unity found in Christ throughout the history of the church.

In the early 17th century, the Puritans escaped religious persecution in England by sailing to the New World. When they arrived, they encountered the native population. Being influenced by the Reformer, Calvin, the Puritans were secure in the knowledge that they were God's chosen people. From their perspective, the native people were not God's chosen and were to be treated as such. Those who so recently had been persecuted in England became the persecutors. The division created by their theological outlook affected not only their evangelistic activities with the native population but

4. Paulson, "Luther Quotes."
5. Luther, *The Jews*.
6. Jewish Library, "Luther Quotes."

also the way the Puritans treated them socially and politically. As God's chosen, the Puritans believed they had the right to dominate other cultures and religions. Later when people with differing religious views immigrated to Puritan controlled areas of the New World, they too were chastised and separated.

The list of divisions and separations, and the evil they inspired, is endless. The whites—sincere Christians that they were—subjugated an entire race of people that they judged inferior and enslaved them. Even after emancipation, and one hundred years later, the civil rights movement of the sixties highlighted that divisions still exist and there is a separation between what is, at least in the judgment of some people, the righteous and the unrighteous; the good and the bad.

Divisions are worldwide, existing from the class system of the United Kingdom to the caste system of India. Though united by a holy book, the "People of the Book"—Jews, Christians, and Muslims—are deeply separated. Nations war against nations. Old-timers unite against newcomers. Sports fans are devoted to a common sport yet separated by their loyalties to their local or regional teams. Family feuds rage like the legendary Hatfields and McCoys.

Certainly, all of these divisions are caused by a multitude of reasons and not just the separations caused by hell and the threat of eternal damnation. There is the tribalism humankind inherited from our Neolithic ancestors. Economic differences, geographical locations, opposing political and theological views—all add to the fray. These all, however, reflect the divisions inherent in the belief in hell and eternal punishment. Those two concepts inspire the dualism of the righteous versus the unrighteous and the good against the bad. All run contrary to the gospel of Jesus Christ, which boldly proclaims we are all children of God. Our unity can be more powerful than what seeks to pull us apart. Our unity, which is ours through the life, death, and resurrection of Jesus, can overcome all of our separations and bring us together again.

WE ARE ALL GOD'S CHILDREN—ALL INCLUDED IN CHRIST'S WORK ON THE CROSS

A universal trait among Christians is our tendency to limit God. We don't believe God can do what God said God would do. Several places in Scripture clearly state that God's purpose in the life, death, and resurrection of Jesus, was the salvation of the whole world. With our acknowledgment that there is no hell and eternal damnation, we understand salvation does not mean to be saved *from* hell, but rather being saved and reconciled *for* our relationship with God.

The author of John's gospel records Jesus sharing this truth in his late-night conversation with Nicodemus. Jesus says, "For God so loved the world that he gave his only Son, so that everyone who believes in him may not perish but may have eternal life. "Indeed, God did not send the Son into the world to condemn the world, but in order that the world might be saved through him" (John 3:16–17). Later, in his letters to the young communities of faith, the author writes, ". . .he is the atoning sacrifice for our sins, and not for ours only but also for the sins of the whole world" (1 John 2:2), and "We have seen and do testify that the Father has sent his Son as the Savior of the world" (1 John 4:14). A similar view is shared in the letter of 1 Timothy where it is written, "This is right and is acceptable in the sight of God our Savior, who desires everyone to be saved and to come to the knowledge of the truth.

> For
> there is one God;
> there is also one mediator between God and humankind,
> Christ Jesus, himself human,
> who gave himself a ransom for all" (1 Tim 2:3–6).

The writer reiterates this point later in his letter writing, "For to this end we toil and struggle, because we have our hope set on the living God, who is the Savior of all people, especially of those who believe" (1 Tim 4:10).

After his survey of the Bible and its references to God's love and desire that all will be saved, Boyd Purcell, a proponent of "Universal Effectual Atonement" writes, "The ever-loving, blessed Holy Trinity truly acts in perfect harmony: God, the Father, created all people; God, the Son, died for all people; and God, the Holy Spirit, seeks the salvation of all people with saving grace which ultimately proves to be irresistible. All people will therefore, be saved!"[7]

The majority of people who identify themselves as Christians, though, don't believe that God is capable of accomplishing God's will. It is easy to see why there is this propensity towards unbelief. Christians have been taught for centuries that it won't happen. It may be God's intention that all will be saved, but in God's dealings with humankind throughout the millennia, God has realized the rebelliousness of God's creation. Admitting defeat, God has been forced to construct in creation a place for hard-hearted, stiff-necked people who refuse God's love and resist God's will.

---

7. Purcell, *Without Insanity*. 88.

Another point that supports the argument that God is incapable of accomplishing God's will is the presence of evil in the world. Evil is all around us. Though we'd like to think that the good guys always win, there are uncountable examples of evil being rewarded and righteous people paying the price. We call for justice. We have also identified being just as a characteristic of God, and we believe that God echoes our cries for justice. Therefore, we reason, God's sense of justice will overwhelm God's desire for the salvation of all. In eternity, justice will be served. The evil, unrighteous people who prospered in their physical lives will suffer horribly and eternally in their life after death. We, of course, will be saved, because we are righteous believers who seek to do God's will in our lives. We're the good guys.

Finally, in our popular theology, there is nothing greater than our free will—not even God's will. Look at what happened in the Garden of Eden! God created a perfect place for humankind. God provided for all of Adam and Even's needs and they walked in a relationship with God. All God asked them to do was to not eat of the fruit from the tree of the knowledge of good and evil. They could munch on everything else, but not the fruit from that tree. Adam and Eve rebelled against God's instructions. Tempted by the serpent, they ate the fruit from the forbidden tree. God couldn't make them obey. Humankind's free will was greater than the will of God. Because of their rebellion, God kicked them out of the Garden of Eden, caused the woman to have pain in childbirth, and condemned the man to hard labor.

From that time, the greatest power in the universe (at least in this world) is humankind's free will. The Lord cannot make us believe in God. The Holy Spirit cannot make us do God's will. We are free to mess up our lives and the lives of many others, and God can't do anything about it. Reluctantly, God yields God's will to our rebellious will and allows us to thwart God's divine purpose for our lives. We condemn ourselves to eternal punishment and God can't do anything about it.

Thankfully, God breaks out of the theological box we have constructed for God. Nothing is greater than God's steadfast love, overwhelming grace, and unconditional forgiveness. God has not admitted defeat and created a place for eternal punishment. Though the Lord seeks justice and calls on believers to strive for justice in the world, God does not allow the desire for justice to pervert God's love or sidetrack God's will for all to live in a relationship with God. Yes, our free will is a powerful force, but it is not more powerful than God's will and love. God's love does not allow us to condemn ourselves to an eternity of punishment.

It is inherently dangerous to anthropomorphize God—to make God into our image. Still, this is one of the only ways that we can conceive of God. The Bible often identifies God as our Father (or parent). We are identified as God's children and together we are the family of God. With this in mind, and acknowledging its limitations, let's look at universal salvation from the point of view of the family.

The love of parents is imperfect—there isn't a parent alive who doesn't feel a sense of guilt over his or her limitation to love his or her children perfectly. (Sadly, there are also times when parental love is severely limited, absent, or replaced by evil.) Parental love is supposed to mirror God's love for us, and most of the time it does. Who else but a loving parent (or grandparent) would put up with tending to an earache in the middle of the night? Only someone who loves a child completely would endure changing a smelly, disgusting dirty diaper. Love is what motivates parents to attend countless hours at teacher meetings, chauffeur their children to innumerable extracurricular events, and cheer their children on in those events.

There are times when children don't reciprocate their parents' love. Requests to clean their rooms, to help wash the dishes, or to take out the trash are ignored. The teenage years, when the emerging adults seek to separate themselves from their parents and establish their own identity, can be especially trying. At times, psychological struggles, social challenges, or addictions arise to test the depth of parental love. Pain and heartbreak, joy, celebration and pride, worry and fear, relief and thanksgiving are all a part of being a parent. During the time of being a parent, it is extremely rare for parents to cast one of their children out of the house and sever their relationship with that child. If we don't condemn our children to a life of homelessness on the streets, why do we think God would cast God's children out of God's presence and condemn them to everlasting punishment—no matter what they did?

There are no bounds to God's love. We see that over and over again in both the Hebrew Scripture and the New Testament. The Israelites were constantly rebelling against God and following false gods and idols. God punished them and sought to bring them back to God. God never gave up on the people of Israel. In the New Testament, Peter denied Jesus three times. Jesus forgave Peter and made him one of the leaders of the early church. Paul persecuted Christians and was responsible for the imprisonment and death of many of them. Still, God moved in Paul's life, brought him to faith, called Paul to spread the gospel into Gentile lands, and inspired Paul to be one of the greatest theologians of the Christian church.

God does not give up on people. It is not just a select few that retain God's love. God doesn't give up on anyone. "God so loved the world that he gave us his only Son . . ." (John 3:16). Jesus lived, died, and rose again so that all might be saved and that none might be condemned. We are all God's children. All of us—no matter our nationality, race, age, color, sex, sexual orientation, gender identification, or whatever else identifies us—are loved by God. And nothing—absolutely nothing—can separate us from God. When Jesus sends his disciples out into the world to baptize and make disciples of all nations, he promises them, ". . . I am with you always, to the end of the age" (Matt 28:20).

No one is condemned to an eternity of torment, pain, and separation from God. All of us have been reconciled to God through the life, death, and resurrection of Jesus. We are all children of God and we are united and not divided. Together we take up the ministry of Jesus to share God's love and grace and to proclaim that Good News.

THE PATH TOWARD MINISTRY AND DIALOGUE—ALL ON EQUAL FOOTING

Life will be different without the constant threat of hell and God's wrath. Imagine what life would be like if love, grace, and forgiveness were in abundant supply. Picture a reality where all people experience God's presence in their everyday lives. Envision a world where people focus on their commonalities rather than their differences. When we do this, we begin to see glimpses of heaven—a heaven on earth.

The first place where we need to experience the differences of life without hell is in our own lives. We have lived our entire lifetimes carrying heavy burdens of guilt and shame. "At the core of our beings," we tell ourselves, "we are no good. We constantly sin against God. There is nothing that we can do to please God. We deserve God's punishment and to experience God's wrath." The conversations we carry on with ourselves may be more or less theological. What they have in common is that they focus on our faults rather than our strengths, are negative rather than positive, and put us down rather than build us up.

Much of life is viewed as reward and punishment. If we receive a promotion or a raise at our place of employment, it is obviously a reward. We are receiving the fruits of our hard work. If our sons or daughters are placed on the dean's list, not only are they being rewarded for their academic achievements, but we pat ourselves on the back for being good parents.

When our car has a flat tire on the freeway during our morning commute, however, we view it as a punishment. We ask ourselves, "What have I done to deserve this?" God might be telling us that we shouldn't have cut that car off in traffic. Or, if we really think about it, the price of getting the tire fixed will be about the same amount of money as we could have given to support a homeless shelter. We should have given the money to the homeless shelter and then we could have avoided the flat tire during our morning commute.

Putting ourselves down, in our conversations with ourselves, is a common experience. Much of it stems from the fact that we believe that we deserve God's wrath instead of God's love. Such thinking is diametrically opposed to the message proclaimed to us in the life, death, and resurrection of Jesus Christ. Going through life celebrating God's love is vastly different than living our lives in fear of God's wrath. Several of the psalms show us what such a life would be like. One of them is Psalm 136.

The history of the Israelites, as it is recorded in the Hebrew Scriptures, is an ongoing relationship with God. Psalm 136 is a celebration of that relationship. The psalm is antiphonal. In the first half of each of the psalm's verses, a leader recites an action of the Lord. The congregation responds to each action by proclaiming, in the second half of the verse, "The steadfast love of the Lord endures forever." The psalm begins with creation. It continues through the Israelites enslavement in Egypt, their journey through the wilderness and their settlement in the Promised Land.

The history of the Israelites was filled with triumph and tragedies. The people suffered greatly in Egypt and they cried out to the Lord to free them. God's love was steadfast. God heard them and called Moses to lead God's people out of slavery. Because of God's steadfast love for the Israelites, the Red Sea was split, they endured the wilderness and won victories over their enemies. In the good times and in the bad times, the one constant in the lives of the Israelites was the steadfast love of the Lord. The Psalm ends:

> "It is he who remembered us in our low estate,
> For his steadfast love endures forever;
> And resued us from our foes,
> For his steadfast love endures forever;
> Who gives food to all flesh,
> For his steadfastlove endures forever.
> O give thanks to the God of heaven,
> For his steadfastlove endures forever" (Ps 136:23–26).

Like the Israelites, no matter what happens in our lives today, there is one constant: The steadfast love of the Lord endures forever. In our promotions, raises, and the achievements of our children, the steadfast love of the Lord is a central part of our lives. In our flat tires, failures, sicknesses, and struggles, God's steadfast love is still at the very core of our beings.

Without hell and damnation, we can bask in God's love. Most of us can remember the time when we first realized someone else loved us. It could have been our parents or another family member but, usually, it was a "significant other." That discovery that we were loved brought a deep sense of peace into our lives. Everything was right with the world, whether we were rich or poor, struggling or thriving. Some of us have had the joy of a child or grandchild throwing their arms around us and declaring to us, "I love you." At that moment, everything seems to be in alignment and the world feels right. Human love and divine love transform our lives. John, in his first letter to the early Christians, wrote, "There is no fear in love, but perfect love casts out fear; for fear has to do with punishment, and whoever fears has not reached perfection in love" (1 John 4:18). We may never love or be loved "perfectly." The more we celebrate the lack of God's wrath and the steadfast nature of God's love, however, the more we can face life—all of life—courageously and without fear.

Paul's exhortation to the Christians in Philippi to "not worry about anything," has puzzled many Christians. Worry is assumed to be a "given" of life in the modern world. Paul's full instruction to the Philippians reads, "Rejoice in the Lord always; again I will say, Rejoice. Let your gentleness be known to everyone. The Lord is near. Do not worry about anything, but in everything by prayer and supplication with thanksgiving let your requests be made known to God. And the peace of God, which surpasses all understanding, will guard your hearts and your minds in Christ Jesus" (Phil 4:4–7).

God's steadfast love is what gives us the ability to live without worry. We are like children who grow up in a loving home. Those children don't worry about food, shelter, or clothing. All of those items will be provided by loving parents. The children enjoy the love of the parents and can experience a carefree life.

God's love is what grants us the peace of God that surpasses all understanding too. Life may not turn out the way we want. Hardships may be commonplace for us. Yet, God's love is constant. As we journey through life, it is God's steadfast love that gives us hope and encouragement and enables us to endure and overcome whatever we may face. Secure in God's love we are at peace.

When she was 38 years-old, Brigit O'Brien was diagnosed with metastatic breast cancer. The disease was in an advance stage and aggressive treatment was indicated. Brigit had a double mastectomy and endured weeks of radiation and months of chemotherapy. To say the least, those days were not easy for Brigit. She did not go through her "hell on earth" alone, though. She was surrounded by her family and friends. Brigit also had a strong faith in God.

Her faith assured her of God's love and provided Brigit with a sense of peace in the middle of the treatments and turmoil.

There were those times when Brigit wanted to scream at the top of her lungs and complain about the unfairness of life. At other times, Brigit fell into deep depressions. She was so sick and weak for some time, she could only exist. Occasionally, Brigit feared that she would not survive. Her family and friends were present with her. They held her hand, wiped her forehead, and offered her sips of water. They listened to her rant and rave and hugged her when she cried. Brigit's family and friends were an expression of God's presence. They gave her strength and hope when she ran out of those commodities.

Several times Brigit was overwhelmed with fear. It would come to her late at night, usually when she was alone. Fear was close by when Brigit was so weak and in so much pain that she almost longed for death instead of life. In those times, Brigit would repeat the words, "Into your hands I commend my spirit." She would surrender to God's love and a feeling of peace would stream into her life. God's love casts out fear.

The absence of hell and damnation and the presence of God's love and grace not only transform our lives, but they also transform our relationship with others. We have developed the habit of looking for people's differences. Once we identify those differences, we use them to determine whether the person is to be included or excluded. We ask ourselves, "Is the person righteous or unrighteous, good or bad, desirable or undesirable?" Putting away these old habits, we can now focus on the truth that the person is a child of God.

The two young cousins, Eddie and Lynn, had it right and serve as a positive example for us. Even though their churches and the adults in their lives told them they were different, they chose to focus on their similarities. They were family who enjoyed playing together.

Imagine the difference it would have made for Kiersten and the other young people at the seminar if they had been able to celebrate their similarities, rather than concentrate on their differences. The youth from Pentecostal and non-denominational congregations might have learned about baptism, communion, and liturgical worship. Such knowledge most certainly would have led to a broader understanding of the Christian church and could have deepened their appreciation of their own religious heritage.

Kiersten might have been able to be exposed to speaking in tongues and other gifts of the Holy Spirit. There is the possibility that she could have been exposed to a different understanding of Christian discipleship and how other people define "holiness." Together the youth could have discussed how they could reach out to their peers and involve their friends, neighbors, and schoolmates in the lives of their congregations. Or, they could have shared missionary trip experiences—encouraging each other with their stories of the experience of God's Spirit flowing through them to touch the lives of the people they went to serve and how the needs of these people were met. Rejoicing that they were all children of God, who were loved by God and used by the Holy Spirit to share God's love and grace, would have added to the richness of their conference and the time they shared. In turn, the church as a whole could have benefited from the unity the youth might have developed.

Kiersten and the other youth could have experienced an ecumenical movement on a personal scale. Ecumenism has been happening across a broad spectrum of Christian denominations. It has been a major force in the Christian church during the last half of the 20th century and into the 21st century. The realization that we are more alike than we are different was the spark that ignited the ecumenical fire.

PATH TOWARD DIALOGUE—ALL ON EQUAL FOOTING

The Lutheran Church and the Roman Catholic Church have been having ongoing dialogues for over fifty years. These conversations enable the two church bodies to issue the Joint Declaration on the Doctrine of Justification (JDDJ) in 1999. "This document intended to show that both the Lutheran and Roman Catholic Church could articulate a common understanding of our justification by God's grace through faith in Christ"[8] This issue was at the heart of the Protestant Reformation.

In another church document, the Lutheran Church and the Roman Catholic Church were able to state: "We are united as Christians by our baptism into Christ. We are taught by Scripture and tradition and share a common life in Christ. We affirm as Lutherans and Catholics in the dialogue process a commitment to the goal of full communion, even as we recognize that further agreements are necessary before full, sacramental communion can be restored."[9]

In 1999, the Evangelical Lutheran Church in America adopted the *Called to Common Mission,* and entered into an ecumenical relationship with the Episcopal Church. The Episcopal Church adopted this document at its General Convention in 2000. In the introduction to the *Called to Common Mission*, the denominations agree that "We therefore understand full communion to be a relation between distinct churches in which each

8. ELCA, *Frequent Questions.*
9. Almen and Sklba, *The Hope,* Preface.

recognizes the other as a catholic and apostolic church holding the essentials of the Christian faith."[10] The ELCA and the Episcopal Church did not proclaim that they were identical and therefore they could work together. In fact, they agreed they were diverse organizations. Still, their unity—that the members of these two denominations were all children of God, enabled them to come together for a common ministry. As a representative of the denominations involved in the ecumenical movement, the ELCA has reached similar agreements with denominations in the Reformed tradition and also with the Methodists. The focus of these agreements is always on our likenesses as children of God and not on our differences as human institutions.

While there is a great incentive for denominations to focus on our unity as Children of God and continue the ecumenical movement, there are also forces present that seek to pull us apart. There is a great divide between the more fundamental branches of the conservative evangelicals and what has been called mainline Protestantism. The differences that are focused upon are political agendas and interpretations of Scripture. Two denominations were formed when the ELCA voted to ordain people who are LGBTQ and living in committed relationships. The Episcopal Church struggles over similar differences and the United Methodist Church may no longer be united because of differences in addressing LGBTQ concerns. A movement to narrow these divisions will only come when we stop separating ourselves into righteous/unrighteous, good/bad, right/wrong, or saved/unsaved, and we acknowledge that we are all children of God who are all loved by God.

CELEBRATE DIVERSITY—GOD'S KINGDOM COMES

The unity that has been rediscovered by many branches of Christianity can also be experienced between different faiths. In many communities, ministerial associations are expanding their membership. Where once they included clergy from various, selected Christian denominations, they now have representation from Jewish, Muslim, Buddhist, Sikh, Hindi, and other faiths. Religious leaders have the opportunity to build relationships with others from different backgrounds and diverse faiths. Efforts are being made to dismantle the walls that have been erected over the decades and centuries and instead build bridges that expand understanding and community.

Several Christian congregations have responded to the Islamophobia that has spread through much of North America and Europe, by inviting representatives from the Islamic faith to speak to their members. The purpose of these informational meetings is to gain a greater understanding of

10. ELCA, *Common Mission*.

Islam's teachings, traditions, and practices. Participants have experienced not only a better understanding of Islam but also an increased comprehension of their own Christian beliefs and how they compare to other faiths. There is also the realization among those gathered that extremists, regardless of their faith backgrounds, can misuse use holy books, like the Qur'an and the Bible, for their own evil, violent purposes.

Religious communities have come together to serve the towns and cities in which they are located. In the aftermath of horrendous wildfires in the western states of the United States, congregations, synagogues, mosques, and temples joined forces and worked together to ease the suffering and meet the needs of their friends and neighbors. Community food banks, soup kitchens, clothing outlets, and shelters are supported by a variety of faith communities.

Different faiths have learned to serve each other. In 2018, two women and their three children vandalized a mosque in Tempe, Arizona. The reaction of the interfaith community in response to the vandalism was overwhelming. Kristy Sabbath, the office manager at the Islamic Community Center of Tempe stated at the time, "The mosque continues to receive phone calls, emails, and Facebook messages from people expressing their solidarity. Interfaith allies are also sending the center flowers and sweets. Many have even brought their children to the Islamic center with handmade cards of love and encouragement.[11] The interfaith community also sponsored a "Love and Coffee" event that over two hundred people attended.

On October 27, 2018, a lone shooter entered the Tree of Life Synagogue in Pittsburgh, Pennsylvania. The shooter killed 11 people, in what was the deadliest act of antisemitism in the United States. In the aftermath of the massacre, support poured out for the survivors and victim's families. Some of that support came from the Muslim community. Within a short amount of time, two Muslim organizations raised over $200,000.00.[12] Previously these Muslim organizations had raised $136,000 to repair hundreds of Jewish headstones that had been vandalized in St. Louis and Philadelphia.[13] Tarek El-Messidi, a Chicago-based activist, was the organizer of these two fundraisers. When interviewed, he stated, "Putting our religious differences or even our political differences aside, the core of all of us is that we have a shared humanity. We really wanted to reach out as human beings to help."[14]

11. Kuruvilla, "Vandalized Arizona Mosque."
12. Haag, "Muslims Raise Money."
13. Haag, "Muslims Raise Money."
14. Haag, "Muslims Raise Money."

Our common humanity and our unity as children of God enable us to bridge gaps and work together for the benefit of all.

Of course, until recently this unity and commonality have not been the case (and for many, it still isn't). Christians, in the past, have understood the Bible to contain the absolute truth. An old Sunday school ditty declared, "The Bible said it. I believe it. That's good enough for me!" There is also Jesus's statement, "I am the way, and the truth, and the life. No one comes to the Father except through me" (John 14:6). Many Christians interpret the word *truth* to be the orthodox doctrines of the Christian Church. These would include such doctrines as the virgin birth, the divinity of Jesus, and his sacrificial death on the cross. The word *way* is understood to be the passage from this earthly existence into God's presence. Life in heaven and God's eternal presence becomes the obvious meaning to the word, *life*.

Armed with the Bible, and standing firm on Jesus's words, Christians believed that we had a franchise on truth. As possessors of the truth, Christians were the people who had been set apart; we were the new Chosen Ones. Not only were Christians the ones who had been blessed, but people from other faiths had been cursed. Without the truth—without Jesus—those people were condemned to hell, eternal punishment, and separation from God.

There is a different way to interpret the words of Jesus that are recorded in John's gospel. The *truth* is Jesus's proclamation that God is a God of love. Motivated by that love, God sent Jesus to be the savior of the world (1 John 4:14), so that no one would be condemned (John 3:17). The *way* is described by Jesus in his summation of the Ten Commandments—to love God and to love our neighbor (Matt 22:37, Luke 10:27). Or, by Jesus's command to his disciples to love one another as he has loved us (John 13:34). The life Jesus talked about is moved from the future to the present. *Life* is the lifestyle of living in the reality of God's love, responding to God's love with gratitude and service, and sharing that love with one's neighbors. With this interpretation of John 14:6, Jesus's words become inclusive rather than exclusive.

Christians are not the only people to believe we were the sole possessors of the truth. People from other faiths believed that they were the ones who had been given the truth. Dialogue is difficult, if not impossible, when each group believes they are the only ones who have the truth. Those who have the truth don't like to listen. They tend only to have an affection for speaking. As followers of Jesus, we might not be able to change another faith's understanding of truth. We can, though, enter into conversation with people of other faiths determined that the conversation will be dialogue instead of a monologue.

The reality that there is no Hell and no one is condemned to eternal punishment changes the dynamics of Christians' interactions with people of other faiths. The truth that we are all God's children, and God's chosen ones, allows us to acknowledge our unity, celebrate our diversity, and discuss our differences. As children of God, we can share the truth that has been revealed to us, while at the same time listening to the truth others have been given. When this occurs, truth is not subtracted from, but rather it is added to, the discussion and our lives. Dialogue does not divide the truth—it multiplies it. This is happening more and more in organized conversations between faiths. Dialogue is happening daily on a personal level.

Lamar Jackson experienced an interfaith dialogue when his wife was killed in an automobile accident. He had been married for 35 years and Lamar's grief was great. He sought help and support from several sources through his journey of grief. Lamar spent time in conversation and prayer with the pastor of the Lutheran Church where he worshiped. On a few occasions, Lamar had worked with a counselor and therapist. In his grief, he sought out the services and support of the counselor, who was Jewish. In their times together, Lamar was able to share the struggles and challenges that he faced and his counselor was able to reflect on them from the perspective of his Jewish faith. Lamar's next-door neighbor and good friend was a Muslim. In their conversations together, during games of golf and around a backyard fire pit in the evenings, Lamar's friend was able to offer support and share insights from his faith. A Buddhist co-worker helped Lamar develop the practice of meditation as a tool to usher in calm to his sometimes-tumultuous life. Lamar remained a Christian, but he was helped through this most difficult time in his life by the spiritual insights of several faiths.

The purpose of interfaith dialogue is not to create one super, all-inclusive faith. Rather, it is to live out the truth that we are all children of God and to learn from each other. There is the potential that we will all be able to grow in our ability to share God's love and grace with each other and to serve our neighbors together. It could at least be hoped that we would be able to stop killing each other for religious purposes.

The absence of Hell and eternal punishment, along with the reality that we are all children of God, has the potential to transform our relationships with people outside our normal social circles. In the late 18th to early 20th century, the Christian church in North America and Europe sent thousands of missionaries to developing nations. The missionaries' purpose was to proclaim the gospel of Jesus Christ to the native people—to save them from hell and damnation. Great things were accomplished. The gospel of

Jesus Christ was brought to the four corners of the world and Christianity became the largest religion in the world. The missionaries built hospitals to heal the sick and schools to educate the populace. In their quest to share the gospel, though, the missionaries spread European and North American culture while at the same time decimating the culture of the native people. Some missionaries may have grieved over this destruction. Others believed it was the necessary price to pay to keep the native people out of Hell.

Compare the actions of those missionaries over the course of two centuries with the ministry of Mother Teresa in the mid to late 20th century. This Albanian sister religious traveled to India. Though she was a Christian, her goal was not to convert the people of India to Christianity, but rather to care for the sick and dying of the lowest castes in Indian society. Mother Teresa simply wanted to share God's love with the people and not allow them to die alone and unloved.

Mother Teresa approached her ministry from a different perspective than that of countless missionaries. Hers was not an emphasis on saving them from hell and eternal punishment (her personal thoughts on the reality of hell and damnation are unclear). Mother Teresa wanted to share the message of Jesus Christ, spread God's kingdom and demonstrate God's love to those she came to serve. To do this, she accepted them as people loved by God. Mother Teresa respected their faith traditions. Her goal was not to change them, but rather to work within them. Mother Theresa's ministry touched the lives of millions and left its mark on the world.

FAMILY FEUDS—DISAGREEMENTS AND JUSTICE

We celebrate the fact that Jesus ushered in the kingdom of God by his life, death, and resurrection. We are all children of God and we no longer need to fear God's wrath or the threat of hell and eternal condemnation. Now, we would like to experience heaven on earth. Unfortunately, evil still exists in the world. There are wars, poverty and hunger, and a host of injustices. Humanly speaking we may be children of God, but we still have a propensity to be self-centered, selfish, and to hurt other people.

Living in a relationship with God is a life-changing experience. God's presence, in the person of the Holy Spirit, is at work in our lives. Paul writes to the Galatian Christians and declares that evidence of the Spirit's work in the lives of Christians is what he calls the fruit of the Spirit. That fruit is love, joy, peace, patience, kindness, generosity, faithfulness, gentleness, and self-control (Gal 5:22–23). During his life on earth, Jesus declared that his followers needed to turn from their self-centered and selfish ways. Jesus said, "If any want to become my followers, let them deny themselves and take up their cross and follow me" (Mark 8:34). There is also the Parable of the Judgment of Nations in Matthew 25, where Jesus clearly points out that his followers are to care for others. In that parable, which takes place at the end of time, the Son of Man calls out to the righteous people and says:

> Come, you that are blessed by my Father, inherit the kingdom prepared for you from the foundation of the world; for I was hungry and you gave me food, I was thirsty and you gave me something to drink, I was a stranger and you welcomed me, I was naked and you gave me clothing, I was sick and you took care of me, I was in prison and you visited me.' Then the righteous will answer him, "Lord, when was it that we saw you hungry and gave you food, or thirsty and gave you something to drink? And when was it that we saw you a stranger and welcomed you, or naked and gave you clothing? And when was it that we saw you sick or in prison and visited you?" And the king will answer them, "Truly I tell you, just as you did it to one of the least of these who are members of my family, you did it to me (Matthew 25:33–40).

FAMILY FEUDS—STANDING FOR JUSTICE

Not only is it necessary for us to feed the hungry, but we also must stand against the injustices that perpetuate poverty and hunger. Visiting those who are in prison is an important ministry. It is also important for us to seek just laws and to make sure that those who are imprisoned are not innocent. The pastor, theologian, and martyr, Dietrich Bonhoeffer, has written, "We are not to simply bandage the wounds of victims beneath the wheels of injustice, we are to drive a spoke into the wheel itself."[15] By doing this, we are not only sharing our love for others, but we are also serving God.

In the past, we have characteristically transformed those with whom we have disagreed into villains. We have demonized those whom we perceived to be the sources and causes of injustices. These tactics may have been useful in uniting the masses against our opponents and in storming the walls of unrighteousness. Now, they are no longer consistent with our world view. Everyone, no matter their political party, religious affiliation, race, nationality, sexual orientation, or gender identity, is a child of God. Their words and actions may disgust us. The harm they cause to other people or parts of creation may alarm and anger us. Still, in God's eyes, and

15. Crosswalk, "Bonhoeffer Quotes."

it would be hoped in our eyes, they are viewed as children of God—people whom God loves.

The question before us, now that we live in the truth of God's love instead of the lie of God's wrath, is, "How do we serve those in need and stand against injustice." There are two Christian leaders (among many others) who serve as examples of standing against evil and injustice while holding onto common humanity. They are Martin Luther King and Dietrich Bonhoeffer—men who struggled against injustice and evil in the most tumultuous of times.

It would have been easy for Martin Luther King to have become bitter and violent in his opposition to the racism he encountered in the southern United States (and in the rest of the United States as well). The segregation of the South had kept millions of African Americans in poverty, denigrated them daily, provided them only a second-class education, and prevented them from having a voice in the communities in which they lived. Many had responded with violence and suffered the consequences. King certainly was under pressure from several sources to become violent in the resistance he and his allies organized. He never yielded to that pressure and temptation. On the topic of nonviolence, King wrote:

> Nonviolence is the answer to the crucial political and moral questions of our time—the need for mankind to overcome oppression and violence without resorting to violence and oppression. Civilization and violence are antithetical concepts . . . Sooner or later all the people of the world will have to discover a way to live together in peace, and thereby transform this pending cosmic elegy into a creative psalm of brotherhood. If this is to be achieved, man must evolve for all human conflict a method which rejects revenge, aggression, and retaliation. The foundation of such a method is love.[16]

Supporters of segregation responded violently to King's demonstrations, protests, and acts of civil disobedience. Members of King's movement and others denounced those who enforced segregation and opposed their efforts. Losing sight of the common humanity they shared with their oppressors, African Americans spoke in a derogatory manner and sought to demonize those of the establishment. King never stooped to that level. He understood that violence and hate would not achieve the goal that he sought. On the subject of violence, King wrote, "The end of violence or the aftermath of violence is bitterness. The aftermath of nonviolence is reconciliation and the creation of a beloved community. A boycott is never an

16. King, "Nobel Peace Prize."

end within itself. It is merely a means to awaken a sense of shame within the oppressor but the end is reconciliation, the end is redemption."[17]

Dietrich Bonhoeffer was one of the few voices in Germany speaking against Hitler and the Nazi government. A pastor and theologian, Bonhoeffer was by nature a nonviolent man. Eventually, though, he came to the belief that Hitler needed to be eliminated to save the world from further violence and bloodshed. Bonhoeffer became actively involved in a plot to assassinate Hitler. The plot failed, and eventually, Bonhoeffer was executed. In his struggles against the tyranny of the Third Reich, Bonhoeffer never lost sight of the love God has for God's creation. He writes, "God loves human beings. God loves the world. Not an ideal human, but human beings as they are; not an ideal world, but the real world. What we find repulsive in their opposition to God, what we shrink back from with pain and hostility. . . This is for God the ground of unfathomable love"[18]

Bonhoeffer gave his life in his opposition to Hitler and the Nazis. He took a stand when the church in Germany did not. Bonhoeffer was very critical of the church in Germany because it either kowtowed to the whims of the Fuehrer, allowing Nazi Fascism to infiltrate the church, or remained silent in light of the Nazi atrocities. It would have been easy for Bonhoeffer to become judgmental and condemning, but he resisted the temptation. "Judging others," he writes, "makes us blind, whereas love is illuminating. By judging others we blind ourselves to our own evil and to the grace which others are just as entitled to as we are."[19]

Life without hell is different—very different. We have lived for such a long time under the threat of hell and eternal punishment. But hell is no longer; in reality, it never was. No longer do we live in fear of judgment and condemnation. We can now live in the reality of God's love. The artificial divisions that have separated us for eons are bridged with the truth that we are all God's children and our common ancestry unites us.

Paul writes that "If anyone is in Christ, there is a new creation: everything old has passed away; see, everything has become new!" (2 Cor 5:17). A new life awaits us. We take our first steps with a sense of joy, excitement, and anticipation. We may not be sure what lies ahead, but we do know that we will be embraced by God's love and empowered by the presence of God's Spirit. Come what may, we have nowhere to go but up!

17. Carson, *Essential King*, 26.
18. Crosswalk, "Bonhoeffer Quotes."
19. Crosswalk, "Bonhoeffer Quotes."

Epilogue

It had been three years since Lydia visited the town where her brother and his family lived. Though her last visit was memorable with the baptism of her nephew, she hadn't been attracted to the community. Though typical small-town USA, there had been an unsettling, sinister quality to the town. At the town's center was the Malmstad place—the derelict, rundown house and grounds. The site had a history of violence and death. It cast a pall over the rest of the community.

Lydia had intentionally avoided returning to the community. Her brother and his family had visited her a couple of times; she had also joined them occasionally on their sightseeing trips. At the same time, Lydia had been very intentional and creative in fulfilling her vows as a godparent. She had devised several creative ways of being involved in the life of her nephew and in assisting his parents in raising him in the Christian faith.

This return to her brother's hometown was unavoidable, though. She had been honored by her brother and sister-in-law and asked to be the godparent of their newborn daughter. Nothing, not even the Malmstad place, could keep Lydia away from her niece's baptism.

Like before, Lydia found herself antsy and wanting to get some exercise and some fresh air. She volunteered to take her nephew on an outing, pulling him in a wagon while she toured the city. Her initial impression of the town was similar to her previous first thoughts. The town was well-kept, with clean streets, groomed yards, and painted houses. The thought of Lake Wobegon again popped into Lydia's head, and she smiled to herself. Lydia did notice a slight difference from her previous visit. The smiles on the people's faces appeared to be more sincere and their greetings a little more heartfelt. Lydia didn't feel a sense of foreboding as she had before.

Lydia and her nephew stopped at a bakery along the way. The aroma was simply too overpowering. Her nephew wanted a cookie—chocolate chip, of course. Lydia ordered a flavored café latte and three Danish pastries (to be enjoyed with her brother and his wife when she returned to their home). After loading her nephew and his cookie into the wagon, Lydia continued her stroll while savoring her latte. A few blocks later, she came to the intersection of the street that led to the Malmstad place. She had decided that this would be the turnaround point for her little jaunt with her nephew. As Lydia was making the U-turn with the wagon, she glanced down the street and was surprised not to see the haunted hulk of the Malmstad place. In its place was a public park.

Lydia couldn't resist the pull of the park. The green grass, fountains, and families laughing together were too much to resist. Her nephew, catching sight of the swings and slide, encouraged her by chanting, "Swing, swing, swing," and pointing his little finger toward the playground. After parking the wagon near one of the park benches, Lydia pushed her nephew on the swings, watching him climb ladders and swoosh down the slides. They played for almost an hour. When the little boy had finally run out of energy, Lydia placed him back in the wagon and headed back to her brother's home. The little guy was asleep in minutes.

Her brother met her at the door. "What happened?" he said. "We were almost ready to send out a search party."

"I'm sorry, I should have called you. We discovered the park where the Malmstad place used to be and we just had to stop and play on the swings and slides."

"Ah, I thought that might have been the case," her brother said, with a nod of his head and a knowing grin. "How did you like Malmstad Park?"

"It's a lovely park," Lydia exclaimed. We had a wonderful time there. The park was crowded and it looked like everyone was having a great time. What happened to the haunted house, weeds, and rusty fence?"

"The last of the Malmstad clan, who held the deed to the property, died a couple of years ago. She willed the property to the town with the stipulation the town make the land into a park and name it 'Malmstad Park.' No one had a problem granting that request. We held a few fundraisers to purchase the playground equipment and a few other necessities. Voila, we have a park."

"Well, I'm impressed. It is certainly a great improvement over the evil place that was there before. I think I even noticed a change in the town's people. Their smiles seemed genuine and they appeared lighthearted."

"I think you're right. Leveling that old house and building the park has made a difference in the community. No one can make a direct connection, but since the town built the park, a few new businesses have come to town. We're having our own little economic revival. I know that sales are up at the store, and that sure makes me happy."

"The people have a more positive attitude on life. There's less gloom and doom expressed over coffee and sweet rolls at the diner. People aren't so worried about the future. In fact, the phrase that I'm hearing more and more is, "We've nowhere to go but up."

Bibliography

Almen, Lowell G. and Richard J. Sklba, eds. *The Hope of Eternal Life: Lutherans and Catholics in Dialogue XI*. Minneapolis: Lutheran University Press, 2010.

Athenagoras, *Plea for the Christians*. New Advent. http://www.newadvent.org/fathers /0205.htm.

Boyd, Greg. "The 'Christus Victor' View of the Atonement." http://www.gregboyd.org/ essays/essays-jesus/the-christus-victor-view-of-the-atonement/.

Brazen Church. "How & When the Idea of Eternal Torment Invaded Church Doctrine," www.brazenchurch.com, January 3, 2016.

Bright, Bill. "Four Spiritual Laws." http://mesacc.edu/~thoqh49081/handouts/bright. html.

Burnhope, Stephen. *Atonement and the New Perspective: The God of Israel, Covenant, and the Cross*. Eugene, OR: Pickwick, 2018.

Calvin, John. *Institutes of Christian Religion*. 1559

Calvinist Corner. "Five Points of Calvinism." http://www.calvinistcorner.com/tulip. htm.

Carson, Clayborne. *The Essential Martin Luther King Jr.: "I Have a Dream" and Other Great Writings*. Boston: Beacon Press, 2013.

Christian Universalist Association. "The History of Universalism." https://christian universalist.org/resources/articles/history-of-universalism/.

Copeland, Stephen. *Where the Colors Blend: An Authentic journey Through Spiritual Doubt and Despair . . . and a Beautiful Arrival at Hope*. New York: Morgan James, 2019.

Crosswalk.com. "20 Influential Quotes by Dietrich Bonhoeffer." https://www.crosswalk. com/faith/spiritual-life/inspiring-quotes/20-influential-quotes-by-dietrich-bonhoeffer.html

Early Christian History. "The Theology of Hell." https://earlychristianhistory.net/hell. html.

Eaton, Elizabeth. "By the Light." *Living Lutheran* (October, 2018) 14–19.

Edwards, Jonathan. "Sinners in the Hands of an Angry God." https://www.ushistory. org/documents/sinners.htm.

Evangelical Lutheran Church in America. "What is the Relationship between the ELCA and the Roman Catholic Church?" *Worship Resources: Frequently Asked Questions.* https://download.elca.org/ELCA%20Resource%20Repository/What_is_relationship_between_ELCA_and_Roman_Catholic_Church.pdf?_ga=2.122037515.1204434129.1583443167–624258729.1580142995.

———. *Called to Common Mission.* https://download.elca.org/ELCA%20Resource%20Repository/Called_To_Common_Mission.pdf?_ga=2.221703320.1204434129.1583443167–624258729.1580142995.

Farrar, Frederick. *Lives of the Fathers: Sketches of Church History in Biography.* London: Adam and Charles Black, 1907.

Ferwerda, Julie. *Raising Hell.* Rathdrum, Idaho: Vagabond Group, 2014.

Froom, Leroy Edwin. *The Conditionalist Faith of Our Fathers—Volume II.* Silver Spring, Maryland: Review and Herald, 1965.

Girard, Rene. *The Scapegoat.* Baltimore: Hopkins University Press, 1986.

Graham, Billy. "Don't Gamble with Your Life or Your Soul." https://billygraham.org/answer/dont-gamble-with-your-life-or-your-soul/

Got Questions. "What is a Kinsman Redeemer." https://www.gotquestions.org/kinsman-redeemer.html.

———. "What is the Septuagint?" https://www.gotquestions.org/septuagint.html.

Haag, Matthew. "Muslim Groups Raise Thousands for Pittsburgh Synagogue Shooting Victims." *New York Times* (October 29, 2018). https://www.nytimes.com/2018/10/29/us/muslims-raise-money-pittsburgh-synagogue.html.

Hanson, J.W. *Universalism: The Prevailing Doctrine of the Christian Church During Its First Five Hundred Years.* Boston and Chicago: Universalist Publishing House, 1899.

King, Martin Luther. "Noble Peace Prize Acceptance Speech." https://www.nobelprize.org/prizes/peace/1964/king/26142-martin-luther-king-jr-acceptance-speech-1964/.

Kuruvilla, Carol. "Vandalized Arizona Mosque Flooded With Support From Interfaith Allies." *Huffington Post* (March 20, 2018).

Jewish Virtual Library. "Martin Luther—'The Jews and Their Lies.'" https://www.jewishvirtuallibrary.org/martin-luther-quot-the-jews-and-their-lies-quot.

Jones, Tony. *A Better Atonement: Beyond the Depraved Doctrine of Original Sin.* Minneapolis: JoPa Group, 2012.

Liantonio, Richard. "Why Greek Matters Pt. 3." http://www.richardliantonio.com/blog/2012/04/why-greek-matters-part-3-into-the-age-the-meaning-of-eternity-in-the-new-testament/.

Livermore, Jeremy. "Augustine's Philosophical Theology." https://www.apologetics.com.

Lose, David. *Making Sense of the Cross.* Minneapolis: Augsburg Fortress, 2011.

Luther, Martin. "An Introduction to St. Paul's Letter to the Romans." *Luthers Vermischte Deutsche Schriften.* Johann K. Irmischer, ed. Erlangen: Heyder and Zimmer, 1854.

———. *The Jews and Their Lies.* Translated by Martin Bertram. CreateSpace, 2017.

Martyr, Justin. *The First Apology.* New Advent. http://www.newadvent.org/fathers/0126.htm.

McMillen, Jacob. "A Biblical Staple the Bible Never Mentions." http://www.brazenchurch.com/hell-in-the-bible/#more-668.

———. "How and When the Idea of Eternal Torment Invaded Church Doctrine." https://www.gotquestions.org/septuagint.html.

Moody, Dwight L. "Jesus is Savior." http://jesus-is-savior.com/Books,%20Tracts%20&%20Preaching/Printed%20Sermons/DL_Moody/hell.htm.

Paulson, Mikel. "Martin Luther's Quotes About Pope." https://www.paulson1611rd.org/martin-luthers-pope-quotes.html.

Purcell, Boyd C. *Christianity Without Insanity: For Optimal Mental/Emotional/Physical Health*. Charleston: CreateSpace, 2012.

Rohr, Richard. *Falling Forward*. San Francisco: Jossey-Bass, 2011.

———. "The Patristic Period." https://cac.org/the-patristic-period-2018-09-09.

Spong, John Shelby. "Why the Church Invented Hell." https://www.wakingtimes.com/2016/05/12/retired-bishop-reveals-why-the-church-invented-hell.

Sunday, Billy. "Quotes." https://www.azquotes.com/author/14309-Billy_Sunday.

Thomson, Alexander. "Whence Eternity? How Eternity Slipped In." https://thetencommandmentsministry.us/ministry/free_bible/whence_eternity

Vincent, Ken R. "The Salvation Conspiracy: How Hell Became Eternal." http://www.christianuniversalist.org/articles/salvationconspiracy.html.

Wengert, Timothy. "By the Light." *Living Lutheran* (October 2018). 14–19.

Wikipedia. "Divine Comedy." https://en.wikipedia.org/wiki/Divine_Comedy.

———. "Francis of Assisi." https://en.wikipedia.org/wiki/Francis_of_Assisi.

———. "Great Awakening." https://en.wikipedia.org/wiki/Great_Awakening.

———. "Paradise Lost." https://en.wikipedia.org/wiki/Paradise_Lost.

———. "Vulgate." https://en.wikipedia.org/wiki/Vulgate.

Why Christmas. "Christmas Customs." https://www.whychristmas.com/customs/25th.shtm.

Yeshua Before 30CE. "The Church's Development of the Hell Myth." http://30ce.com/deveopmentofhell.htm.